ENERGY
RESOURCES,
UTILISATION,
AND
POLICIES

ENERGY
RESOURCES, UTILISATION, AND POLICIES

J. H. HORLOCK, FRS

Whittle Laboratory
Cambridge University, United Kingdom

KRIEGER PUBLISHING COMPANY
Malabar, Florida
2009

Original Edition 2009

Printed and Published by
KRIEGER PUBLISHING COMPANY
KRIEGER DRIVE
MALABAR, FLORIDA 32950

Copyright © 2009 by Krieger Publishing Company

Library of Congress Cataloging-in-Publication Data

Horlock, J. H.
  Energy : resources, utilisation, and policies / J.H. Horlock. — Original ed.
    p. cm.
  Includes bibliographical references and index.
  ISBN-13: 978-1-57524-299-6 (alk. paper)
  ISBN-10: 1-57524-299-0 (alk. paper)
  1. Power resources. 2. Energy policy. 3. Energy consumption. I. Title.
  TJ163.2.H664 2009
  333.79—dc22
                                                    2008043858

10 9 8 7 6 5 4 3 2

Contents

Preface xi

Acknowledgements xv

Chapter 1
A General Introduction to Energy—Demand,
Reserves, and Use 1
1.1　Forms of Energy 1
1.2　Units of Energy 1
1.3　Primary Energy Supply 3
1.4　Energy Reserves 5
1.5　Renewable Energy 9
　　1.5.1　Biomass 9
　　1.5.2　Total World Use of Renewables 10
1.6　Distribution of Resources 11
1.7　Future Energy Scenarios 11
1.8　The New Environmental Factor—Global Warming 14
1.9　How Energy Resources Are Used 16

Chapter 2
Energy Conversion and the Laws of Thermodynamics 19
2.1　Introduction 19
2.2　Heat and Work 19
2.3　The First Law of Thermodynamics 19
2.4　The Second Law of Thermodynamics 20
　　2.4.1　Absolute Temperatures 21
　　2.4.2　The Carnot Heat Engine 23
2.5　Processes with Chemical Change 24
2.6　Steady Flow 25
2.7　The Efficiencies of Power Plants and Heating Devices 28
　　2.7.1　Definitions of Efficiency 28
　　2.7.2　Maximum Heat—Calorific Value 29

2.7.3 Maximum Work 29
2.7.4 The Efficiencies of Practical Power Plants 30
2.8 Combined Heat and Power 31

Chapter 3
Work (Power) Production—Stationary Power Plants 33
3.1 Introduction 33
3.2 Steam Power Plants 33
3.2.1 The Basic Rankine Plant 33
3.2.2 Measures to Raise the Mean Temperature of
        Heat Supply 35
3.2.3 Calculations of Practical Steam Plant Efficiency 36
3.3 Gas Turbine Plants 37
3.3.1 The Open Gas Turbine Plant 37
3.3.2 The Closed Cycle Gas Turbine Plant and
        the Air Standard (Joule-Brayton) Cycle 38
3.3.3 Calculations of Practical Gas Turbine
        Plant Efficiency 40
3.3.4 Variations on the Simple Open Gas Turbine Plant 41
3.4 Combined Cycle Gas Turbine Plants (CCGTs) 43
3.5 Integrated Gasification Combined Cycle Plants (IGCC) 44
3.5.1 The Basic IGCC Plant 44
3.5.2 Modification of the Basic IGCC Plant 45
3.6 Internal Combustion (IC) Engines 46
3.7 Nuclear Plants 46
3.8 Fuel Cells 48
3.9 Renewable Power Plants 49
3.10 The Financial Cost of Producing Electricity 50

Chapter 4
Heating and Refrigeration Processes 53
4.1 Introduction 53
4.2 Types of Heaters 54
4.2.1 Heaters in Power Plants 54
4.2.2 Industrial Heating Processes 57
4.2.3 Heating in the Commercial Sector 59
4.2.4 Domestic Heating 59
4.3 Novel Heating Systems 60
4.3.1 Heat Pumps 60
4.3.2 Condensing Boilers 61

4.3.3 Renewable Heating Systems 62
4.4 Other Components Involving Heat Transfer or Rejection 62
4.5 Refrigeration and Air Conditioning 62
4.6 Discussion 64

Chapter 5
Combined Heat and Power (Cogeneration) 67
5.1 Introduction 67
5.2 Types of CHP Plant 67
5.3 Performance Parameters for a CHP Plant 70
5.4 The Pass-out or Extraction Steam Turbine 71
5.5 The Back-Pressure Steam Turbine 72
5.6 The Gas Turbine with a Waste Heat Boiler 72
5.7 The CCGT/Back-Pressure Plant 73
5.8 The CCGT/Pass-Out or Extraction Plant 73
5.9 Comparison of Energy Utilisation Factors (EUF)
       and λ_D for Two CHP Plants 73
5.10 The Economics of CHP Plants 73
5.11 Conclusions 77

Chapter 6
Power Plants for Transport 79
6.1 Introduction 79
6.2 The Reciprocating Internal Combustion Engine 80
       6.2.1 The Four-Stroke Engine 80
       6.2.2 The Two-Stroke Engine 81
       6.2.3 Air Standard Cycles 81
       6.2.4 Performance of IC engines 85
6.3 The Turbojet Engine 88

Chapter 7
Pollution and Global Warming 91
7.1 Introduction 91
7.2 The Greenhouse Effect and the Carbon Cycle 92
7.3 Carbon Dioxide Production and the Kyoto Protocol 96
7.4 Actions in the United Kingdom Following Kyoto 98
7.5 Other Countries 99
7.6 Fiscal Methods—Carbon Taxing and Carbon Trading 100
7.7 Carbon Sequestration and Storage (CSS). 103
7.8 The Longer Term 104

Chapter 8
Renewable Sources of Energy 107
8.1   Introduction 107
8.2   Renewable Methods of Heating 108
   8.2.1   "Old" Traditional" Methods 108
   8.2.2   "New" Renewable Methods 108
8.3   Contributions of Renewable Generation 109
   8.3.1   Renewables as a Percentage of All
           Electricity Generation 109
   8.3.2   The Renewables Contribution to Primary
           Energy Supply 111
8.4   Types of Renewable Generation 112
   8.4.1   Energy Crops and Biofuels 112
   8.4.2   Waste 113
   8.4.3   Wind 114
   8.4.4   Tidal 118
   8.4.5   Wave Power 119
   8.4.6   Solar Photovoltaics (PV) 119
8.5   Intermittency 119
8.6   Discussion 121

Chapter 9
Energy Scenarios and Energy Policy 123
9.1   Introduction 123
**9.2   Factors Controlling Energy Consumption and
      Scenario Predictions** 123
   9.2.1   Population and Energy per Capita 124
   9.2.2   GNP and Energy Intensity 124
   9.2.3   Energy Efficiency 125
9.3   Energy Scenarios 125
   9.3.1   For the World—the WEC Scenarios 125
   9.3.2   The WEC Conclusions 126
   9.3.3   Regional and National Scenarios 127
9.4   Energy Efficiency 129
**9.5   Reduction of Primary Energy Demand by
      Increasing Energy Efficiency** 131
   9.5.1   Magnitudes of Possible Savings from Increasing Energy
           Efficiency: The Example of the United Kingdom 133
9.6   The World Scene—Possible Savings 136
   9.6.1   The Princeton "Wedge" Concepts 136

9.7 Discussion and Conclusions 136
    9.7.1 The Stern Report 138
    9.7.2 Conclusions 139

Appendix A
Economics of Power Plants.. 141
A.1 Introduction 141
A.2 Electricity Pricing 141
A.3 The Capital Charge Factor 142
A.4 Example of the Use of the Analysis.................................... 143

Appendix B
Socolow and Lam Analysis 145

Index 147

Preface

Energy has now risen high up on the agenda of the world's problems. For many years, estimates of world energy resources have suggested that they will be adequate to meet the demands of the rich, developed countries. More recently, however, two issues have modified this view.

First, it is apparent that the greater use of fossil fuels, involving the production of carbon dioxide, has increased the CO_2 concentration in the world's atmosphere. It is generally agreed by a substantial majority of climate scientists that this is leading to global warming, a rise in the earth's temperature, with some disastrous consequences probable rather than possible. There will have to be restrictions worldwide on the use of fossil fuels and their production of CO_2.

Second, the rapid expansion of the economies of the developing world, and particularly India and China, means that the world's resources of fossil fuel, particularly oil and natural gas, are now available for much shorter periods.

In 1993, Sir Denis Rooke, Professor Ian Fells, and I organised a conference at the Royal Society on "Energy for the Future," obtaining contributions from several distinguished authors drawn from many countries around the world. In 1995, we published the proceedings in a book (1). This contained a mine of information, inevitably condensed, for specialists in the field, so it was not in a useful form for instruction in the general subject of energy.

Some ten years later, my former colleagues at the Open University (OU) wrote a course entitled "Energy for a Sustainable Future" (a successor to a much shorter and earlier OU course on energy), and they subsequently produced three excellent "books of the course" (2,3,4). These contained comprehensive material for their students and indeed for the general public who could obtain these very large books of the course.

My purpose in writing this book is to produce a reasonably short book lying between the concentrated specialist Royal Society book and the wider comprehensive OU volumes. I hope that in this form it may be used as a text for single-term general courses on energy for engineering and science students, but that it may also be suitable for high school students and members of the general public with a modest scientific background.

The nature of energy is first discussed, and in particular, the "bound" chemical energy available to us in the fossil fuel reserves and in uranium. A simple presentation of the conservation of energy (the first law of thermodynamics) follows, together with discussion of the conversion of bound chemical energy into useful forms of energy, that is, heat and work. The limitations of the second law of thermodynamics are indicated.

The mechanisms of conversion of "chemical energy" into useful form, in power plants for work and in heating devices for useful heat, are then described. The utilisation of combined power plants to produce both work and useful heat is explained.

The implications of the dangers of CO_2 production in power plant design are briefly explored. The virtues of carbon sequestration and storage are emphasised, particularly for coal-fired plants.

The attractions of using renewable resources to produce work and heat are discussed, including brief descriptions of various renewable sources (wave and tidal, solar, biomass, etc.). A fuller discussion of the most promising form of renewable generation, wind power, is included.

To conclude the book, options that are possible for the reduction of both fossil fuel usage and CO_2 production, now available technologically, are presented within a brief discussion of energy scenarios and policies—national, European, and worldwide.

In writing this book, I am conscious that I have had to give limited presentations of subjects, which in themselves merit much fuller and more detailed attention, indeed, very often separate text books. For example, it has not been fully possible to develop logically all the corollaries of the Second Law of thermodynamics—these alone may require a full textbook for their presentation (e.g., Montgomery [5]). Similarly the complexity of the relationships between fossil fuel energy use, carbon dioxide formation, resulting atmospheric concentrations and consequent global warming are the subjects of worldwide study and massive literature production at present. I have attempted to present simple statements of the results of these studies, as agreed by most members of the relevant scientific community.

However, I have learnt the need for rigour in engineering scientific writing from my mentors, Keenan (6) and Shapiro at Massachusetts Institute of Technology (MIT), and Hawthorne and Haywood (7,8) at Cambridge. So although my presentations are necessarily brief and simplified, I have tried to make sure that they do not contain inaccurate statements.

In presenting the studies of energy consumption and dwindling reserves,

I am aware that it is a fast-changing scene that I have tried to summarise. The data I have used are obtained from many places (sometimes via the Internet) and do not always read across easily or precisely from one set to another. The World Energy Council and the International Energy Agency form the major sources of information and British Petroleum annual statistics have also been up-to-date and valuable. These various sources are appropriately referenced at the end of the relevant chapters.

I am open to the criticism that the energy picture will be different in, say, ten to twenty years from now. But in this area, time is short, so there is a strong case for writing down the present position since action is required relatively quickly. That action should not only rely on an assessment of the most important current data but also on a community educated in energy resources and utilisation. It is that community that I have hoped to help in writing this short book.

I am indebted to many colleagues for useful discussion, criticism, and help. The list includes Professor Ian and Alastair Fells (of Fells Associates), Professor John Young of Cambridge University, Professor Harvey Lam of Princeton University, Professor Michael Laughton, now Emeritus Professor at Imperial College, and Professor Hongde Jiang, of Tsinghua University, Beijing. Dr. Godfrey Boyle has also been generous in the provision of OU material, by himself and several colleagues.

Advancing years and occasional illness have slowed down and interfered with the writing of this book, but I have been helped enormously by Dr. Budimir Rosic, Research Fellow at my old laboratory, the Whittle, in Cambridge. He has not only assisted in the production of simple, elegant figures but has also been helpful in critical reading of the text.

I am also indebted to Mr. Robert Krieger (and associates in his company) for publishing this book. He has republished five of my previous books, enabling them to be widely read in America. This first publication of *Energy: Resources, Utilisation, and Policies* continues a happy association that has lasted over forty years.

Finally, I must again record my thanks to my wife, Lady Sheila Horlock, for her patience and forbearance in dealing with a husband frequently absent in his study, with his books, and his computer. Yet again, for the eighth time, I promise her that this is the last book I shall write, but this time I really will not break my promise after a few years!

J. H. Horlock
Cambridge, United Kingdom 2007

References

1. Rooke, D., Fells, I., and Horlock, J. H. [ed.], 1995, *Energy for the future*, Chapman and Hall, London.
2. Boyle, G. [ed.], 2003, *Energy systems and sustainability*, Oxford University Press, Oxford.
3. Boyle, G. [ed.], 2004, *Renewable energy*, Oxford University Press, Oxford.
4. Watson, J. [ed.], 2007, *Managing transport energy*, Oxford University Press, Oxford.
5. Montgomery, S. R., 1966, *Second law of thermodynamics*, Pergamon Press, Oxford.
6. Keenan, J. H., 1941, *Thermodynamics*, John Wiley, New York.
7. Haywood, R. W., 1980, *Equilibrium thermodynamics*, John Wiley, London.
8. Haywood, R. W., 1991, *Analysis of engineering cycles*, Pergamon Press, Oxford.

Acknowledgements

In presenting these studies of energy consumption and dwindling reserves, I am aware that it is a fast-changing scene that I have tried to summarise. The data I have used are obtained from several places and do not always read across easily or precisely from one set to another. The World Energy Council and the International Energy Agency form the major sources of information and British Petroleum annual statistics have also been up-to-date and valuable. These various sources are appropriately referenced in the text and at the end of the relevant chapters.

J. H. Horlock
Cambridge 2007

Chapter 1
A General Introduction to Energy—
Demand, Reserves, and Use

1.1 Forms of Energy

A detailed discussion of energy begins with definitions of its various forms and the transformation between those forms. A litre of oil (of mass about one kilogram) possesses a quantity of "bound" chemical energy; but such *primary* energy is not useful until it is turned into other forms of useful energy, *heat* in a boiler (e.g., to heat water for warming a house), or *work* (e.g., the electrical work produced in a power station). If the electricity is used to run a one-bar kilowatt electric fire, then the electrical energy is being turned back into heat to warm the house.

The primary energy in the litre of oil cannot be made by man. Oil is a finite resource that is available on the planet having been created naturally over thousands of years from the sun's energy. It can be recovered for use but this recovery requires money and effort.

There is a further source of energy flowing into the earth day-by-day; this is referred to as *renewable* energy in that it comes in continuously from the sun and the earth's motion. It arrives directly as heat and indirectly in the form of air movements (winds) and water movements (waves, rivers, and tides), which can be harnessed to do work. If such continuous supplies of energy can be converted into useful heat or work, then much less of the world's bound or primary energy, a finite resource, needs to be used.

1.2 Units of Energy

Units of energy, work, and heat can be defined similarly as they are transformable, but to an extent which is governed by the laws of thermodynamics that will be discussed in the next chapter.

The unit of energy is therefore defined in terms of the unit of work, the *joule,* which is the work done when a unit force of one newton is displaced through a unit distance of one metre. (The newton is that force that when applied to a body of mass one kilogram, gives it an acceleration of one metre per second per second.)

1

It is also convenient to talk about power, the rate at which energy is used, and the rate at which chemical energy can be transformed into useful heat and useful work. The unit of power is the *watt*, which is a joule per second, and the small electric fire referred to above had a capacity of one kilowatt (one thousand watts). This describes the rate at which it uses electrical work, $\dot{W} = 1$ *kilowatt*, where the dot superscript indicates a rate. In one second, a *kilojoule* of energy would be used, that is, $W = 1$ kilojoule, and in one hour a *kilowatt hour* would be used, $W = 1$ kWh = 3,600 kilojoules.

In statements of the primary energy resources that are available in the world, the kilojoule is not a very convenient unit to use as it is very small. A kilogram of oil has bound chemical energy of many kilojoules (about 45,000), and a tank containing 1,000 litres of oil (about a tonne or a thousand kilograms) would have about 45 million kilojoules. If we had a million such tanks of oil, then we should have an energy quantity equivalent to a million tonnes, or in technical jargon, one Mtoe (a million tonnes of oil equivalent), corresponding to 45 trillion (million million) kilojoules.

In dealing with world energy resources, we use large quantities of energy units and they often involve powers of ten. The standard way of expressing such powers of ten is

10^{18} exa (E), one quintillion
10^{15} peta (P), one quadrillion
10^{12} tera (T), one trillion
10^{9} giga (G), one billion
10^{6} mega (M), one million
10^{3} kilo (k), one thousand

Thus, an EJ of electricity is an exajoule or 10^{18} joules, and a gigatonne of oil equivalent (Gtoe) is 10^{9} tonnes of oil. The main units used in this book to describe energy resources and energy use are EJ, TJ, TWh, Gtoe, and Mtoe.

A conversion table for these frequently used energy units is given in Table 1.1.

The main (large) units used to describe power are MW, GW, and TW. However, in describing the cost of energy, we use smaller units; for example, an electricity cost of cents per kWh or a gasoline cost of dollars per gallon, or euros per litre.

Table 1.1 Conversion Table

	EJ	TJ	TWh	Mtoe	Gtoe
1 EJ =	1	10^6	278	24	24.10^{-3}
1 TJ =	10^{-6}	1	278.10^{-6}	24.10^{-6}	24.10^{-9}
1 TWh =	36.10^{-4}	3,600	1	86.10^{-3}	86.10^{-6}
1 Mtoe =	0.042	42.10^3	11.7	1	10^{-3}
1 Gtoe =	42	42.10^6	$11.7.10^3$	1,000	1

1.3 Primary Energy Supply

The Mtoe is a unit used to express both supply and demand for energy, and the resources available. The word equivalent means that no matter the type of fuel—oil, coal, gas, or uranium—its energy use can be expressed in an equivalent form, that is, of Mtoe. Indeed, in considering the resources there are in the world, it is convenient to use an even bigger unit, the gigatonne oil equivalent (Gtoe), a thousand Mtoe. This is an enormous quantity—many supertankers are required to transport one gigatonne of oil.

Demands for energy in all countries are proceeding apace. Table 1.2 shows the amounts of primary energy the world used in 1990, 1995, 2004, and 2005. The energy used is expressed in the form of primary energy (where the fuel is used directly to obtain heat) or equivalent primary energy (where electricity has been generated). Thus, the numbers listed under nuclear and hydro are obtained from known electrical energy consumption and then making thermally equivalent estimates of primary energy required, usually assuming a "conversion efficiency" of 38% (this being the ratio of electrical work to the primary energy that would have been used in a good conventional power station to generate that electrical work).

The IEA also gives interesting and complex detail of how the total primary energy supply (TPES) becomes the total (energy) for consumption (TFC) in many processes (electrical power generation, crude oil distillation to petroleum products, coal transformation, etc.). The TFC products then include petroleum products, oil gas and coal for heating, and electricity, together with heat from combined heat and power (CHP) plants.

IEA data gives TPES for 2004 as 11.2 Gtoe (if no hydro correction is made), as indicated in Table 1.1, and then show how this is reduced to a TFC value of 7.6 Gtoe, a net reduction (or "energy loss") of 3.6 Gtoe. Much of this reduction is associated with heat wasted in plants producing electricity

Table 1.2 Primary Energy Supply (Gtoe) in 1990, 1995, 2004, and 2005

Form	1990	1995	2004	2005
Coal	2.3	2.3	2.8	2.9
Oil[a]	2.8	3.2	4.0	3.8
Natural gas	1.7	2.1	2.3	2.5
Nuclear[b]	0.4	0.5	0.7	0.6
Hydro[b]	0.5	0.6	0.24/0.38 = 0.63, i.e., when corrected for generation	0.7
Traditional (T)[c]	0.9	—	T + R together = 1.2	—
Renewables (R)[c]	0.2	—		—
Total	8.8	8.9 + T + R	11.6	10.5 + T + R

Sources: For the year 1990, the sources are Rooke, Fells, and Horlock (1995) and The World Energy Council (1993); for the years 1995 and 2005, BP Statistical Review of World Energy (2006); for the year 2004, International Energy Agency (2006).

[a] The figures given here for oil are essentially for crude oil obtained from reservoirs deep below the surface of land or sea. Crude oil contains many species with differing hydrocarbon chain lengths, and their boiling points increase with the chain lengths. In oil refineries, different products can be extracted by distillation in which crude oil is heated and products of differing chain lengths are pulled out. These products, with increasing boiling range, include petroleum gas, naphtha, gasoline, kerosene, gas oil or diesel distillate lubricating oil, heavy gas, or fuel oil, and leave residuals—solids with multiringed compounds with many carbon atoms. Different products are used for different purposes, for example, gasoline for motor cars and kerosene for aircraft jet engines.

[b] WEC and BP take nuclear and hydro figures obtained from known electrical energy consumption and make thermally equivalent estimates of primary energy, assuming a "conversion efficiency" of 38% in conventional power stations. (IEA does not do this for hydro but a conversion has been added in Table 1.2.) Renewable electrical energy is converted similarly by WEC, but BP gives no detailed statistics for renewable energy (see later discussion in chapter 8).

[c] Traditional fuels, such as wood, peat, and animal waste, are important in developing countries. The amount used is difficult to measure and to document. Numbers are not available in the BP reviews; but the energy statistics produced by the IEA (5) show that "combustible renewables, waste and other" totalled about 1.2 Gtoe in 2004. So the total primary energy supplied in the world in 2005 approached 11.7 Gtoe.

in conventional fossil fuel electricity generation plants (it would appear to be some 2.3 Gtoe), but an additional 0.6 Gtoe is given as "own use" including transformations in refineries. Other energy losses include 0.2 Gtoe for coal transformation (e.g., coal to coke) and 0.2 Gtoe for distribution losses, together with miscellaneous small losses.

It is instructive to consider the amount of electricity generated in the world. In total, this amounted to about 63 EJ in 2004 (5). The conversion factor between EJ and Gtoe is 1 Gtoe ≈ 42 EJ so that the electricity *consumption* was about 1.5 Gtoe in 2004, as against about 11.6 Gtoe in total primary energy. Thus, electricity work produced represented some 13% of the world's primary energy consumption in 2004 (a similar calculation showed a slightly lower percentage in 1995).

But these total figures include electricity production by nuclear and hydro. Fossil-fired stations produce 46.7 EJ (1.1 Gtoe). Since on average the world's fossil-fired power stations achieve not much more than 35% efficiency when transmission losses are taken into account, this electrical generation uses nearly three times the electrical work output in primary (fossil) energy consumed, say 1.1/0.35 = 3.2 Gtoe. Most of the balance of about 2.2 Gtoe (3.2 – 1.1) is rejected as the IEA detailed data on energy losses indicated earlier. Some of this "rejected heat" is used usefully for district heating but relatively very little in total across the world, the rest being wasted.

1.4 Energy Reserves

Table 1.2 shows that overall primary energy consumption increased by about a third over the fifteen-year interval between 1990 and 2005, so it would be logical to expect that reserves of primary energy would reduce correspondingly, that is, at an accelerating rate. Assessments of these reserves are usually presented as the proven reserves—"those quantities that geological and engineering information indicates with reasonable certainty can be recovered in the future from known reservoirs under existing economic and operating conditions" (BP's definition [4]).

Estimates of proven reserves (R) of fossil fuels in 1985, 1990, 1995, and 2005 are as listed in Table 1.3 and the distribution between different fuels is shown in Figure 1.1.

An apparent anomaly is that the reserves seem to be increasing over this twenty-year period, but this is explained by realising that more fields are being discovered and that changing economic circumstances may lead to existing fields may be more intensely exploited.

**Table 1.3 Proven Fossil Fuel Reserves (R)
in 1985, 1990, 1995, and 2005 (Gtoe)**

Form	1985	1990	1995	2005
Coal	?	474	?	315
Lignite	?	110	?	143
Oil	105	137	140	164
Natural gas	90	108	129	162

Sources: For the years 1985, 1995, and 2005, the source is BP Statistical Review of World Energy (2006); for the year 1990, the sources are Rooke, Fells, and Horlock (1995) and The World Energy Council (1993).

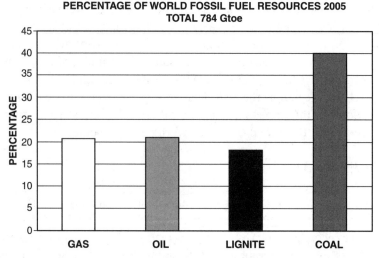

Fig. 1.1. Percentages of World Fossil Fuel Resources by Fuel

The laws of supply and demand mean that annual requirements for the various fuels are met approximately by their known annual production rates (P), since on a world scale there is little storage of useful energy. Then with the proven reserves (R) known, further estimates may be made of the number of years that each fuel would last (R/P). Table 1.4 and Figure 1.2 show two estimates of this R/P ratio for fossil fuels, one made by the World Energy Council for 1990, and one by BP for 2005. (The diagram shows the second estimate graphically.)

The striking thing about this information is that over the fifteen-year period 1990–2005, the "years remaining" (R/P) for oil and natural gas have

Table 1.4 Reserves Production Ratios (*R/P*) for 1990 and 2005

Fuel	*R/P* (1990)	*R/P* (2005)
Coal	197	155
Lignite	293	Not given separately
Oil	40	41
Natural gas	56	65

Sources: For the year 1990, the sources are Rooke, Fells, and Horlock (1995) and The World Energy Council (1993); for the year 2005, BP Statistical Review of World Energy (2006).

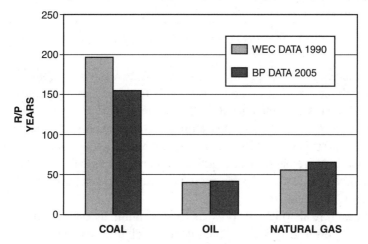

Fig. 1.2. Reserves Production Ratio (*R/P*)

changed relatively little. This is because although energy demands for these fuels have increased substantially, so have the proven reserves for the reasons given above. But these increases in demand will not be matched in the future by the increases in the proven reserves. The WEC and BP estimates of (*R/P*) for coal are again similar but the WEC gave a separate estimate for lignite (soft coal) showing substantial reserves for this fuel (the BP figure for coal apparently includes "sub-bituminous coal").

A more optimistic picture can be drawn from estimates of the "ultimately recoverable fossil fuel reserves, the reserves that can be obtained assuming high but not prohibitive costs of recovery (see Table 1.5 for the WEC estimates).

Now the total reserves rise from about 1,000 Gtoe to over 4,000 Gtoe, with coal and lignite the major resources. The reserves of lignite greatly

Table 1.5 Ultimately Recoverable Fossil Fuel Reserves

Fuel	Gtoe	Percent
Coal and lignite	3,400	76
Conventional oil	200	5
Unconventional oils		
Heavy crude	75	2
Natural bitumen	70	2
Oil shale	450	10
Natural gas	220	5
Total (approx.)	4,400	100

Sources: Rooke, Fells, and Horlock (1995) and The World Energy Council (1993).

enhance the extent of the combined coal and lignite reserves combined, within this overall picture of ultimately recoverable reserves. Similarly, the picture on overall oil reserves changes if the "unconventional" oils are included, the extent of oil shale reserves being dominant. However, this oil is held within impregnated rock, referred to as oil sand or tar sand, and is not easy or cheap to extract. But it remains clear that fossil fuel reserves are finite, and will be used up in a few generations; even coal is unlikely to last beyond the end of the twenty-first century.

The picture also changes if we include uranium, used for the production of nuclear power. Estimates of the rate at which uranium is being used for nuclear power suggest that proven reserves will last for about 40 years, at the mid 1990s rate of consumption, generating about 340 GW and contributing some 0.4 Gtoe (or about 4.5%) to global energy demand and consumption. Ultimately recoverable reserves would extend this rate of provision to some 60 years of operation, in what is called once-through operation in thermal reactors, using slow neutrons.

By 2005, the nuclear contribution had risen to about 0.6 Gtoe, probably still only about 4.5% of global energy consumption, because of limitations on nuclear power development which followed the Chernobyl disaster. But as will be explained in a later discussion of nuclear power, fast reactors, using fast neutrons, can be used to breed more fissile material as well as produce power, and then the potential of the uranium reserves becomes very large indeed. Estimates suggest that the equivalent energy reserves would then be nearly double the total energy reserves of fossil fuels.

1.5 Renewable Energy

A major current debate is whether renewable sources can be expanded to replace our use of fossil fuels and uranium in power plants producing work, and of fossil fuels in heating processes. The principal types of renewable energy listed in Chapter 7 of Rooke et al.'s (1) are given in Table 1.6 with the form of useful energy they deliver.

It is a usual practice today to divide these various types into traditional and new renewables (T and N, respectively). A rather fuzzy line divides the two but an attempt is made to classify the types as T or N, or both, in Table 1.6. Traditional power (work) sources included the first two listed, that is, wind (windmills) and small hydro (water wheels). But these two sources, wind and hydro, are now very much part of today's energy programmes involving new renewables, as wind turbines (and wind farms of many turbines), and as large hydro generating plants.

Other new and feasible renewable power sources are waves and tides, municipal and industrial wastes, and fast-growing crops such as coppiced willow. Photovoltaics—solar power, the direct production of electricity from sunlight—has great attraction for renewable enthusiasts but makes only a very small contribution to world power production as yet. The source is free and infinite but the costs are prohibitive.

In the developing countries, there is a dominant use of traditional energy sources for heating—the use of biomass, which merits a more detailed discussion in the following section. The major use of renewables for heating in the industrialised countries lies in solar designs, passive and active, for domestic housing and offices.

1.5.1 Biomass

Biomass does not appear specifically in the list given in Table 1.6, perhaps because it is an all-embracing term and covers both traditional and new renewables. *Bioenergy* is a general term for energy derived from materials such as wood and animal wastes, which were recently living matter—biomass. The earth has a virtually infinite store of biomass, which, without our intervention, is continuously replenished by the flow of solar energy, and through the process of photosynthesis in plants and trees. This involves absorption of carbon dioxide and discharge of oxygen. But the processes of plant respiration and decay, and possible later combustion, reverse this process, requiring oxygen and producing carbon dioxide. Thus, without inter-

Table 1.6 Principal Types of Renewable Energy

Type	Use
Wind (T and N)	Work
Hydro (T and N)	Work
Wave (N)	Work
Tidal (N)	Work
Municipal waste (N)	Work
Industrial waste (N)	Mainly work
Landfill gas (N)	Mainly work
Special energy crops (N)	Mainly work
Agricultural and forest wastes (mainly T but some N for biofuels)	Mainly heat but some work
Passive solar design (T and N)	Heat
Active solar (N)	Heat
Photovoltaics (N)	Work
Geothermal heat (N)	Heat and work

vention, biomass contributes to the maintenance of the composition of the earth's atmosphere. However, the disappearance of major forests, without reforestation, in several countries (e.g., Brazil) is a matter of great concern in the carbon cycle of the world.

We may capture some of the biomass for use as a fuel. If in burning this fuel to generate useful heat and work no more carbon dioxide is produced than would have been created by the natural processes that we have stopped, then the fuel may be regarded as renewable and its use as a sustainable process.

Traditional biomass, the agricultural and forest wastes, is mainly but not entirely used as a fuel providing heat, particularly in developing countries, and is regarded as renewable. In the industrialised countries, a major new renewable may be the future use of biomass (e.g., sugarcane) in the manufacture of biofuels for use in transport.

1.5.2 Total World Use of Renewables

Table 1.2 showed how in 1990 all renewables (mainly traditional, but also including new ones and large hydro) contributed about 1.6 Gtoe to world primary energy supply, some 18% of the total requirement of about 9 Gtoe. There has been some growth in renewable energy provision over the past twenty years. Data on the use of traditional fuels (such as wood, peat, and animal waste) are unreliably documented but large hydro has risen from 0.5 to 0.7 Gtoe. It is the contribution of newer renewables, from 0.2 Gtoe in 1990, that has since been growing but again their total contribution so far is difficult to assess.

An optimistic ecologically driven WEC estimate (1,2) puts forward a high figure of 1.3 Gtoe for new renewables by 2020. Assuming that the traditional contributions would change little, the total renewable contribution would then be about 3 Gtoe, approximately a quarter of primary demand.

These new renewables will play an important part in reducing both the world's consumption of fossil fuels and its carbon dioxide production. The assumptions made for such development play an important part in predictions of primary energy consumption through the many energy scenarios that have been drawn which we discuss later.

1.6 Distribution of Resources

Another important aspect of the world energy scene is the distribution of resources. Table 1.7 and Figure 1.3 show the distribution of the world's proven resources of fossil fuel, as given by the World Energy Council in 1993 (2).

While coal reserves are distributed across many continents, the major resources of oil lie in the Middle East and the major resources of natural gas are in the Middle East and the old Commonwealth of Independent States (CIS) formed after the split up of the Soviet Union.

In this asymmetry in the distribution of oil and natural gas resources, measured against the major current demands in Europe and the United States, soon to be more than matched by the demands of India and China, lie major problems of security of supply.

1.7 Future Energy Scenarios

So far we have looked at the extent of the resources available to us, and how long they would last assuming recent rates of energy use. However, as the brief discussion in the last section showed, it is by no means a static picture.

As the world's economies expand, so energy demand grows, and the

Table 1.7 Distribution of Fossil Fuel Reserves
(percentage of world-proven total)

	Coal	Oil	Natural Gas
Asia	20	4	6
Australasia	9	—	—
Middle East	—	63	34
Commonwealth of Independent States	23	18	40
Central and Eastern Europe	7	—	—
Organization for Economic Cooperation and Development Europe	10	1	4
North America	24	4	6
Latin America	2	10	6
Other	5	0	4
Total	100	100	100

utilisation of fossil and nuclear fuels will also increase unless renewables come into play on a major scale.

There are many estimates of the possible future patterns of energy demand in the literature, notably those by the WEC. These involve predictions of world population increase, of parallel economic growth, and the way energy is used across the world. Various scenarios are used to make predictions of energy demand, which is based on these various factors; the scenarios include

a. reference cases (B), assuming things go on much as they are doing at present (business as usual);
b. cases (A), assuming a high rate of economic growth;
c. cases (C), which are assumed to be ecologically driven, in which the world makes major attempts to reduce its dependence on energy.

The results of the scenario studies by the WEC in 1993 suggested that on a business as usual basis (B), the annual demand for energy would in-

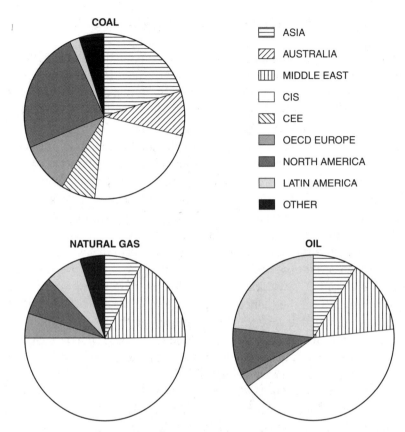

Fig. 1.3. Distribution of Fossil Fuel Reserves

crease from about 9 Gtoe in 1990 to over 13 Gtoe in 2020. For a high growth case (A), it would increase to over 17 Gtoe in 2020; but for an ecologically driven case (C), it could be held to some 11 Gtoe. It appeared then that the demands of the developed Organisation for Economic Cooperation and Development (OECD) countries will change relatively little (and might even decrease somewhat for the ecologically driven case). However, the demand of the developing countries, and particularly India and China, will probably triple and make up about half the world demand by 2020 (or even more than that).

Later work in 1998 by the WEC projected these three forecasts of energy demand forward to 2050 as B (business a usual) = 20 Gtoe, A (growth) = 25 Gtoe and C (ecological) = 14 Gtoe. We do not amplify descriptions of the WEC work here but discuss such scenarios in more detail later in Chapter 9.

1.8 The New Environmental Factor—Global Warming

Historically, the major concerns about primary energy demand (and the associated consumption) have been in relation to how long the world's resources would last. There have been no restrictions placed on demand other than the implicit laws of supply and demand. Money may not be available in a developing country to buy the energy in a particular form and convert it into useful heat or work. Further, as supplies begin to run out, so prices will increase and the cost problems may become more severe and worldwide.

But more recently environmental factors have come strongly into play, and the pattern of solely market-driven supply and demand takes on another form; hence, the introduction of the ecological scenarios into the discussions referred to earlier. These new factors may take the form of somewhat philosophical discussions about conservation, for example, whether forests should be preserved to maintain the diversity of the earth's species. But a sharper argument is now taking place following firm scientific evidence that temperatures on the planet are increasing. It is now widely (but not universally) agreed that such global warming is partly dependent on man's actions in increasing the concentration of the so-called greenhouse gases in the atmosphere (mainly carbon dioxide, but also methane and water vapour), which occur as the result of burning fossil fuels. Table 1.8 shows the world primary energy supplies in 1990 and 2005, together with the carbon emissions (in GtC) and the concentration of carbon dioxide in the atmosphere (in parts per million by volume, ppmv) as given by the World Energy Council (3).

Also shown are the WEC projections of these figures for 2020 (both the high growth scenario and the ecologically driven scenario). Even in the latter case it is clear that the world will be hard pressed to hold down the concentration of carbon dioxide in the atmosphere. The link between global temperatures and these emission figures are less certain, and we do not show the latest estimates here. However, concern over global warming has led to international discussions, negotiations, and a level of agreements (such as that of the Kyoto protocol in 1990, more recently a European agreement in 2007, and attempts at a recent world meeting in Bali) to restrict the output of carbon dioxide (or more simply carbon) and consequent efforts to reduce consumption of useful energy and the demands for primary energy, particularly the fossil fuels.

We discuss these newer restrictions and the required actions in more detail in later chapters, particularly after we have considered in some detail

Table 1.8 Carbon Emissions and Carbon Dioxide Concentrations

Year	1990	2005	2020 (high growth estimate)	2020 (ecologically driven estimate)
Primary energy supply (Gtoe)	9	11–12	17	11.3
Carbon emissions (GtC)	5.0	7.25	11	6.3
Atmospheric CO_2 concentrations (ppmv)	355	380	434	404

how the "bound" chemical energy in fuels is converted into useful form as heat and work. The "thermodynamic" efficiencies of such processes are defined as the ratio of useful heat or work produced to the primary energy input (as in a "boiler" efficiency or a power plant thermal efficiency). Increases in these thermodynamic efficiencies will be required worldwide, but parallel efforts must be made to reduce demand by improving the utilisation of useful energy once it has been produced. This will have to be achieved by many various methods (e.g., by better insulation of buildings so that less heat is required to maintain the same degree of comfort, by switching off electrical equipment on standby, by use of long-life electric light bulbs, reducing electrical power but providing the same degree of illumination, and by major changes in transport practices, such as greater use of public transport such as trains and buses as opposed to individual automobiles, and use of lower carbon fuels). Clearly such actions will also lessen the demand for primary energy, and are just as important as improving thermodynamic efficiencies. Some policy statements loosely refer to the combination of two actions—improving both the performance of the basic conversion process and reducing the amount of useful heat or work that is utilised—as improving energy efficiency.

In the following chapters, we discuss how energy efficiency can be increased with consequent reduction of the primary energy required and the carbon dioxide produced. In Chapters 3–6 we discuss how processes that produce useful heat and work may be made more thermodynamically efficient, or how they might be replaced by renewable systems, but efforts will also have to be made to throttle back demands for both heat and work.

1.9 How Energy Resources Are Used

The use of energy resources to provide useful heat and work is summarised in Figure 1.4, which shows how the energy resources, in their various forms (e.g., P in total), are converted into useful heat and useful work in several ways, to meet the world's demands. The subsequent wastages of energy are not shown.

There are enormous demands for work in our society (more loosely described as demands for power, the rate of supplying work). This is mainly produced from bound chemical energy, in generating electricity and for transportation, but nuclear and hydro are also electricity suppliers. Most electricity, a clean and convenient power source, is produced in large central power stations, using coal, oil, gas and nuclear fuel. This electricity is transmitted and distributed widely at high voltage along electrical grids, for many industrial, commercial, and domestic purposes. But there are other ways of converting the chemical energy in the fuel into useful work, as in smaller local power plants. Some combined heat and power plants provide both distributed electricity generation and useful heat, and we shall describe some of these later. Fuel cells, which convert chemical energy directly into electrical work, are also growing in importance.

About a third of the world's primary energy $(0.33P)$ goes towards providing electrical work $(0.13P)$. Much of the difference goes into heat rejected and is wasted from the power plants (although some is now being converted into useful heat in CHP plants). Electricity is also easily converted into heat, and is then used for warming buildings, a convenient but wasteful practice since such heat could be provided more efficiently by direct heating.

Some 17% of our primary energy $(0.17P)$ goes into producing power for transport, This demand may take the form of electrical power to drive trains, trams, and other transportation, some of which is generated in large central power stations, the rest in smaller power stations and distributed locally at lower voltages. There is also a dominant demand for the production of direct local power, produced by internal combustion engines to drive cars, buses, trucks and lorries, and gas turbine engines (turbojets) to propel aircraft. The convenience of the transportability of liquid fuels (oil products such as diesel fuel, petroleum, and kerosene) is vitally important for the production of this direct power, but a large part of the primary energy used again goes into wasted, rejected heat, much in the form of exhaust gases from the portable power plants.

Most of the rest of the world's primary energy, up to 50% $(0.5P)$, is used

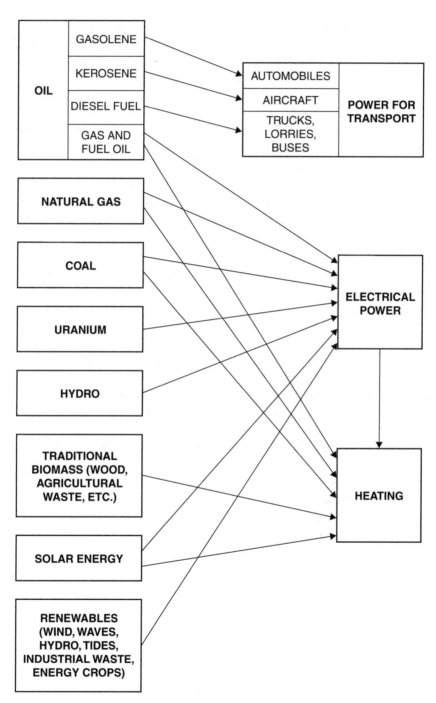

Fig. 1.4. Energy Resources—Useful Heat and Work

in the conversion of fuel directly to heat. A very large part of the world, outside the developed countries, relies on traditional renewable biomass sources (wood and agricultural waste, etc.) for its energy, most of which is used in heating and cooking. Of the world's annual energy consumption (P), this traditional use of our resources represents about 10% ($0.1P$), a surprisingly large percentage.

In the developed and developing countries, industry requires heat, for manufacturing and chemical processes; this heat is usually provided in boilers and furnaces fired by fossil fuels. In addition, heat is also required for commercial, domestic, and industrial buildings to maintain the comfort in which we work and live; this heat is mainly provided in boilers producing steam, hot water, or hot air for central heating and it is again fossil fuels (coal, oil, and natural gas) that are usually used.

The role of the new renewables is also indicated in Figure 1.4 for generating electricity (waves, wind power, tides, industrial waste, and hydro) and for supplying heat (solar power).

References

1. Rooke, D., Fells, I., and Horlock, J. H. [ed.], 1995, *Energy for the future*, Chapman and Hall, London.
2. The World Energy Council, 1993, *Energy for tomorrow's world—The realities, the real options and the agenda for achievement*, Kogan Page, London.
3. The World Energy Council, 1998, *Energy for tomorrow's world—Acting now*, London.
4. BP Statistical Review of World Energy, 2006, *Quantifying energy*, British Petroleum, London..
5. International Energy Agency, 2006, *Key world energy statistics* (data for 2004), Paris.

Chapter 2
Energy Conversion and the Laws
of Thermodynamics

2.1 Introduction

In the first chapter, we explained that bound "chemical energy" in a fuel may be converted and then used as other forms of energy, useful heat and useful work. Here we consider such transfers in more detail. This will involve a simple discussion of the laws of thermodynamics for a system—a fixed quantity of matter within prescribed boundaries across which matter does not pass—but the reader is referred to standard text books on thermodynamics, such as Keenan (1), Gyftopoulos and Beretta (2), Haywood (3), Rogers and Mayhew (4), Moran and Shapiro (5), and Montgomery (6) for fuller discussion. (Texts 2–6 all rely on Keenan's early volume.) We shall find that taking a system through a cycle, letting it pass through various states, but eventually returning to its original state, enables us to transform heat into work on a continuous basis.

2.2 Heat and Work

Heat and work must first be more precisely defined: *heat* is an energy transfer in which energy flows from a high temperature to a low temperature; and *work* is an energy transfer, which could be replaced by the raising or lowering of a weight. The definition of work is precise but not very illuminating. We shall meet several forms of work: *Mechanical* work resulting from movement of the boundaries of a system, for example work done by a piston in an internal combustion engine on the engine crankshaft; *Shaft* work, such as that done by a rotating turbine on an electrical generator; *Propulsive* work, that done by an aircraft engine propelling a vehicle; *Electrical* work, that done by an electric current.

2.3 The First Law of Thermodynamics

The laws of thermodynamics describe the transfer of heat and work to or from a system in thermodynamic processes. In its simplest form, the

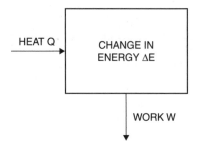

Fig. 2.1. First Law of Thermodynamics

First Law states that for a closed system energy cannot be created or destroyed.

A more rigorous statement refers to a thermodynamic system, a fixed quantity of matter with defined boundaries (Figure 2.1). Then the First Law says that the increase in the energy of a system (ΔE) is equal to the net amount of heat Q added to the system (the difference between the heat supplied Q_B and the heat rejected Q_A), less the amount of work done by the system (W) on its surroundings, so that

$$\Delta E = (Q_B - Q_A) - W \qquad [2.1]$$

If the system undergoes a cycle then it returns to its original state, with its original properties (including the energy) unchanged. Then $\Delta E = 0$ so that

$$(Q)_{CY} = Q_B - Q_A = (W)_{CY} \qquad [2.2]$$

This analysis can describe a cyclic heat engine receiving and rejecting heat and producing work. We measure the cycle efficiency of such an engine (η_{CY}) as the ratio of the useful work obtained to the heat supplied, that is,

$$\eta_{CY} = (W)_{CY}/Q_B = (Q_B - Q_A)/Q_B = 1 - Q_A/Q_B \qquad [2.3]$$

The cycle efficiency is sometimes called the thermal efficiency but we shall not use that term here or subsequently.

2.4 The Second Law of Thermodynamics

The Second Law of Thermodynamics may be expressed in several ways. Montgomery (6) gives nine statements of the Law, but here we quote only two, named after their originators.

a. *Clausius*. It is impossible to construct a device that, operating in a cycle, will produce no effect other than the transfer of heat from a cooler to a hotter body. (Or put more colloquially, but not by Clausius, one cannot cook a kipper on ice!)

b. *Kelvin-Planck*. It is impossible to construct a cyclic heat engine for which the only external effects are the transfer of heat to it from a single thermal energy reservoir and the transfer from it of an equivalent amount of work. (Or the efficiency of a continuously operating cyclic heat engine cannot attain 100%, with zero heat rejection.)

For an engineer, the second of these statements is perhaps the more useful form. It is an empirical statement, which essentially says that it is not possible to achieve a perfect heat engine, that is, one completely transforming heat into work. Such a perfect heat engine is sometimes referred to as a perpetual motion machine of the second kind, a PMMSK. (A perpetual motion machine of the first kind, a PMMFK, is an engine that would produce work without any heat supply at all.) The engineer's proof of the Second Law is that no one has ever made a PMMSK, let alone a PMMFK!

An important concept that arises in discussion of the Second Law is that of reversibility. A system undergoes a reversible process if that first process can be effaced, that is, it can be completely wiped out. This means that a second process can be devised in which both the system and its environment are returned to their original states; the internal energy of the system is completely restored and the original heat and work transfers to or from the environment are completely reversed. The original reversible process is an ideal, virtually perfect process, and a heat engine is reversible if each of its heat and work processes can be reversed.

2.4.1. Absolute Temperatures

A corollary of the Second Law leads to the definition of an absolute temperature scale (T). This corollary is not derived here and the reader is referred to other texts (1–5) for such a formal derivation. Here we shall simply relate T to a more familiar temperature scale derived from a constant volume gas thermometer (see Figure 2.2a).

If the temperature of the bulb containing the gas (A) is changed, the volume of gas, for example, hydrogen, can be kept constant at B by raising or lowering the right arm containing the manometric fluid, mercury. The gauge pressure p_g, that measured above atmospheric, is found from the level

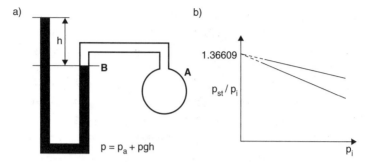

Fig. 2.2. Constant Volume Gas Thermometer.
a, Pressure measurement; and *b,* Steam/ice point pressure ratio

of the containing mercury and the associated height *h* shown in Figure 2.2a, that is,

$$p_g = \rho_m g h \qquad [2.4]$$

where ρ_m is the density of mercury.

The absolute pressure *p* of the gas is then found by adding the gauge pressure to the known atmospheric pressure p_a,

$$p = p_a + p_g = p_a + \rho g h \qquad [2.5]$$

A temperature scale τ is then defined, proportional to the absolute pressure,

$$\tau = ap \qquad [2.6]$$

where *a* is a constant. In particular the ratio *r* of the steam-point temperature (*st*) to the ice-point temperature (*i*) is then

$$r = p_{st}/p_i = \tau_{st}/\tau_i \qquad [2.7]$$

The experiment can be repeated after removing some gas from the bulb and the pressure ratio *r* determined again. After a series of such experiments, *r*, effectively a temperature ratio, can be plotted against the ice-point pressure p_i as indicated in Figure 2.2b; a straight line results that can be extrapolated back to zero ice-point pressure p_i. The limiting value of *r*, as p_i goes to zero, is found,

$$\lim(r)_{p_i \to 0} \tau_{st}/\tau_i = 1.36609$$

If the experiment is repeated with a different gas, for example, nitrogen, then another straight-line relationship is derived, but with the same limiting value of 1.36609, as shown in Figure 2.2b.

If the difference between the steam point and the ice-point temperatures is taken as 100 degrees, as on the centigrade scale, then

$$(\tau_{st} - \tau_i) = 100°,$$

From these two conditions, it then follows that $\tau_{st} = 373.16°$ and $\tau_i = 273.16°$.

It can be shown, (1–6), that this temperature scale τ is identical to the absolute scale T, which is derived from a corollary of the Second Law, $\tau \equiv T$, with the temperature zero on this scale at $-273.16°C$, on the centigrade scale.

2.4.2 The Carnot Heat Engine

Another corollary of the Second Law refers to a reversible heat engine based on the Carnot cycle. In this particular cycle, this heat engine receives all its heat Q_B from a thermal reservoir B at the top "absolute" temperature T_B and rejects all its heat Q_A to a thermal reservoir at the lowest "absolute" temperature T_A. It may then be shown that

$$(\eta_{CY})_{CARNOT} = W_{cycle}/Q_B = (Q_B - Q_A)/Q_I = (T_B - T_A)/T_B. \qquad [2.8]$$

Again we give this result without proof, referring to the listed texts (1–6) for formal derivation.

The Carnot efficiency is the highest cycle efficiency that can be achieved between given temperature limits of heat supply and heat rejection. Equation [2.8] illustrates that even a Carnot engine cannot attain 100% efficiency, because an absolute temperature of heat rejection of zero, $T_A = 0$, cannot be achieved.

Equation [2.8] is vitally important to the engineer because it gives an objective (the Carnot efficiency) to strive for in designing cyclic heat engines, for given maximum and minimum temperatures, T_B and T_A. In practice most of the heat supplied to a real power plant (a practical heat engine) is at a temperature below the maximum T_B and most of the heat rejected by the engine is at a temperature above the minimum T_A. These heat transfer processes are not then reversible (technically they are said to be "externally irreversible"). The other processes making up the cycle may or may not be reversible (they may be internally reversible if they do not involve contact with external thermal reservoirs). However, practical power plants are not cyclic heat engines, and before we consider the efficiency of such real power plants, we must consider both chemical change and steady flow processes.

2.5 Processes with Chemical Change

The discussion of energy (E) so far has not included any reference to the bound "chemical energy" discussed in the first chapter; but E embraces such energy. Consider a small amount of the litre of gasoline discussed in Chapter 1, but now suppose that some has been sprayed into a cylinder with a piston at one end (Figure 2.3), containing sufficient air to enable the fuel to burn with the oxygen therein (combustion). The liquid droplets of fuel occupy only a small fraction of the total cylinder volume, the air occupying most of the volume. Combustion may be initiated by a spark, but in this almost instantaneous nonflow process, it is supposed that there is initially no transfer of heat or work to the surroundings. Then, from the First Law, it follows that there has been no change in energy in this process (ignoring the small quantity of energy added in the spark). But what has happened is that the products of combustion are much hotter than the original "reactants"—the fuel and air which were at a low temperature—say the temperature of the environment. The products are also at a higher pressure, the volume having remained approximately constant in what is called "constant volume combustion." The total internal energy of the contents has not changed, but there has been a transfer of chemical energy of the reactants into the "thermal energy" of the products.

Next heat could be transferred out of the closed system, now at high temperature, perhaps to cooling water in a jacket surrounding the cylinder.

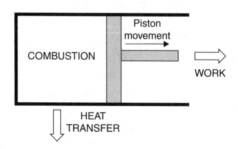

Fig. 2.3. Combustion and Work Processes

We could allow work to be done by the piston, letting it move outwards slowly against a restraining force.

In these actions we would have produced two processes that could be used in an elementary *power plant* (the constant volume combustion process and the working stroke of an internal combustion engine) in which heat is rejected and work is produced.

However, the processes just described could not be used in a cyclic heat engine. The product gases could not be returned to the initial state of the fuel and air making up the reactants; this is because of the chemical change in the combustion (which is not a reversible process but is irreversible).

But we are not only interested in engines to produce work. Converting chemical energy into useful heat alone is another vital requirement for society. The gasoline or oil could be burnt with air at constant volume (i.e., constant energy) to form high-temperature gas, just as in the first of the processes just described, without any work transfer. Now the cooling water in the cylinder jacket, heated up by the hot gases formed by the combustion of the fuel and air, could supply useful heat externally, perhaps for central heating to warm our house. Or the heat from combustion in many similar cylinders could supply "district heating" on a larger scale, say in a block of apartments.

These processes are hypothetical rather than really practical and as indicated before could not be used precisely and directly in a real heat engine. But they contain elements that may be paralleled in real power plants.

2.6 Steady Flow

The processes discussed in the preceding sections are " nonflow," referring to "closed" systems in which the amount of matter does not change, although its composition may alter. But most practical engineering devices processes involve "steady flow," rather than nonflow.

We can imagine a "control surface" (CS) surrounding a device through which passes a system (S)—a fixed quantity of fluid matter—as illustrated diagrammatically for time t in Figure 2.4. But as an elementary part of S shifts a small way into the control surface during time dt, another elementary part is discharged out of CS. Another identical system S' now occupies the original position of S. As a result, conditions within the control surface (and the fluid properties of the fluid measured at any point) do not change with time.

We can still apply the laws of thermodynamics to the system S, which receives heat dQ and does work dW in time dt, but may develop the first law

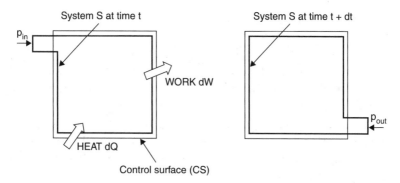

Fig. 2.4. Flow of System S Through a Control Surface

equations to give new "rate" equations for the control surface CS (sometimes confusingly referred to as an "open system"). The rate of heat and external work transfers to and from the control surface are then $\dot{Q} = dQ/dt$ and $\dot{W} = dW/dt$. But "flow work" (a form of displacement work) is required from the system S to push the elementary part out of the control surface and flow work is received by the system S in receiving the elementary part from the environment. If the mass of the two elements entering and leaving the control surface is dm, then the volumes pushed in and out are $v_{in}dm$ and $v_{out}dm$ respectively where v represents the local specific volume, the volume per unit mass. The flow work quantities required are $p_{in}v_{in}dm$ and $p_{out}v_{out}dm$ and these do not appear as external work. They are absorbed into a new system property called the enthalpy, $h = u + pv$, where u is the "thermal energy" per unit mass. Then the statement of the first law for the flow through the control surface is

$$\dot{Q} - \dot{W} = \dot{m}(h_{out} - h_{in}) \qquad [2.9]$$

where $\dot{m} = dm/dt$ is the flow rate through the control surface.

We can apply this equation to the steady flow through any defined control system, including the various components of a steady flow "cyclic heat engine," one in which a circulating fluid undergoes a series of heat and work processes before returning to its original state. For example, in a cycle called the Rankine cycle (Figure 2.5), water (in state 1) is first heated in a boiler, turns into steam (in state 2) which then passes through a steam turbine, delivering work in driving an electrical generator. The steam (now in state 3) then enters a condenser where heat is rejected to cooling water. Finally the condensed water (in state 4) is pumped up to boiler pressure, work being supplied to drive the feed pump, and the water can then enter the boiler

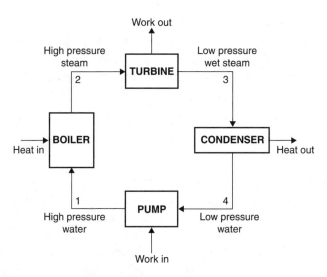

Fig. 2.5. Rankine Cycle

again in its original state (1).

Referring to Figure 2.5, Equation [2.9] can be supplied to a control surface surrounding the boiler,

$$\dot{Q}_B - \dot{W} = \dot{m}(h_2 - h_1) \qquad [2.10]$$

where $\dot{Q}_B = dQ_B/dt$ is the rate of heat supplied in the boiler. Similarly, for the turbine, condenser, and feed pump, the corresponding equations are

$$\dot{W}_T = \dot{m}(h_2 - h_3) \qquad [2.11]$$

where $\dot{W}_T = dW_T/dt$ is the rate of work output from the turbine,

$$\dot{Q}_A = \dot{m}(h_3 - h_4) \qquad [2.12]$$

where $\dot{Q}_A = dQ_A/dt$ is the rate of heat rejection from the condenser; and

$$\dot{W}_P = \dot{m}(h_1 - h_4) \qquad [2.13]$$

where $\dot{W}_P = dW_P/dt$ is the rate of work supplied to the feed pump.

These four equations may then be summed to give

$$\dot{Q}_B - \dot{Q}_A = \dot{W}_T - \dot{W}_P \qquad [2.14]$$

which is the steady flow energy equation for the large control surface surrounding the whole Rankine cyclic heat engine.

The efficiency of this steady flow cyclic heat engine is then

$$(\eta_{CY})_{RANKINE} = \frac{\dot{W}}{\dot{Q}_B} = \frac{\dot{W}_T - \dot{W}_P}{\dot{Q}_B} = \frac{(h_2 - h_3) - (h_1 - h_4)}{(h_2 - h_1)} \qquad [2.15]$$

There are several types of practical power plants, which are essentially steady flow cyclic heat engines and some of these will be described in the next chapter. Other power plants (such as the reciprocating internal combustion engines) operate on a series of nonflow processes. But the mass flow through such an engine measured over a large number of successive identical cyclic operations is averaged over that period and the plant is treated as though it is steady.

2.7 The Efficiencies of Power Plants and Heating Devices

2.7.1 Definitions of Efficiency

Practical power plants and boilers use fossil fuels as a source of energy and most operate under steady flow conditions; air and reactants are supplied and product gases formed by combustion are discharged continuously.

The thermodynamic arguments applied to cyclic heat engines do not apply directly for most practical power plants and a different concept is used to assess their performance.

For a power plant the rational efficiency (η_R) is defined as the ratio of the useful work obtained to the maximum work that could be obtained from the bound energy of the fuel used,

$$\eta_R = \dot{W}/\dot{W}_{max} . \qquad [2.16]$$

The problem then is finding the maximum work $\dot{W}_{max}$.

For a heating device a large proportion of the bound chemical energy in the fuel is transformed into a heat supply but no work is extracted. Another concept of efficiency is used as a measure of its performance (η_B)—a heating device or boiler efficiency (η_B). It is defined as the ratio of the useful heat transferred $(\dot{Q}_U)$ to the maximum heat that could be transferred in an isothermal combustion process $(\dot{Q}_U)_{max}$,

$$(\eta_B) = \dot{Q}_U/(\dot{Q}_U)_{max}, \qquad [2.17]$$

and now the problem is to find the maximum heat $(\dot{Q}_U)_{max}$.

The determination of $(\dot{Q}_U)_{max}$ and $\dot{W}_{max}$ is neither obvious nor easy, but here we give a simplified approach to the problem.

2.7.2 Maximum Heat—Calorific Value

The quantity $(\dot{Q}_U)_{max}$ may be determined from a calorific value measurement, an experiment in which unit mass of fuel is burnt with air at constant atmospheric pressure. The process is cooled to maintain the temperature (usually atmospheric) of the reactants supplied (fuel and air) and the gases produced (Figure 2.6). There is no work output or input so the First Law (in the form of the steady flow energy equation) gives the amount of heat abstracted as $H_{in} - H_{out}$, where H_{in} is the total enthalpy of the reactants (fuel and air) entering and H_{out} is the total enthalpy of the products leaving. This quantity is called is called the calorific value (CV), per unit mass of the fuel supplied, and is a measure of the bound chemical energy of the fuel.

Then for a flow rate $\dot{f}$ of fuel supplied to a boiler the maximum heat that could be obtained is

$$(\dot{Q}_U)_{max} = \dot{f}(CV) \qquad [2.18]$$

and this can then be used in the expression for the boiler efficiency, that is,

$$(\eta_B) = \dot{Q}_U/(\dot{Q}_U)_{max} = Q_U/\dot{f}(CV). \qquad [2.19]$$

2.7.3 Maximum Work

The First Law was used to determine the maximum heat that could be obtained in a real steady flow isothermal combustion process with no work output. Determination of the maximum work requires application of the Second Law, to study a perfect "reversible" change from reactants to products, all at the same pressure and temperature—usually environmental conditions [see the referenced texts (1–6)]. It is often found that the maximum work does not differ much from the maximum heat transferred in the calorific value experiment, that is,

$$\dot{W}_{max} \approx \dot{f}(CV). \qquad [2.20]$$

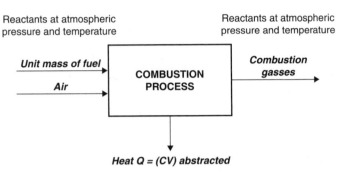

Fig. 2.6. Calorific Value Experiment

It is therefore common practice to define an (arbitrary) overall efficiency for an "open" power plant as

$$\eta_O = \dot{W}/\dot{f}(CV) \qquad\qquad [2.21]$$

rather than use the more precise but complex rational efficiency definition. After Haywood (3) we shall follow that practice, but note that again η_O is sometimes referred to as a thermal or thermodynamic efficiency, a practice that will be avoided here.

2.7.4 The Efficiencies of Practical Power Plants

A practical power plant with external combustion (Figure 2.7a) may involve both a steady flow cyclic heat engine and a heating device burning fuel to supply heat to the engine. The cyclic heat engine has substantial heat losses and its thermal efficiency cannot attain anything like unity—the more heat is lost, the lower its efficiency. Similarly, the heating device has a boiler efficiency less than unity because it also loses heat.

In a steam power plant, a boiler of efficiency $(\eta_B) = \dot{Q}_U/\dot{f}(CV)$ is used to supply heat $\dot{Q}_U$ to a Rankine closed cycle heat engine of cyclic efficiency $(\eta_{CY})_{RANKINE} = (\dot{W}/\dot{Q}_U)$. The overall efficiency of the complete steam power plant is then

$$(\eta_O) = \dot{W}/\dot{f}(CV) = (\eta_B)(\eta_{CY})_{RANKINE}. \qquad\qquad [2.22]$$

This may be of the order of 40% in a modern steam plant with over half the bound energy in the fuel supply lost in the form of unused rejected heat from both the cyclic Rankine cycle (with $[\eta_{CY}]_{RANKINE} \approx 0.45$) and the boiler

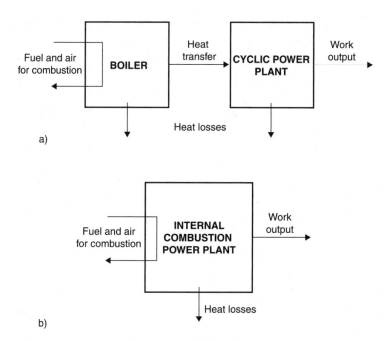

Fig. 2.7. *a*, Power Plant with External Combustion, and
b, Internal Combustion Power Plant

(with $[\eta_B] \approx 0.9$). We give more details of the efficiency of steam power plants in the next chapter.

A gas turbine internal combustion plant converts bound chemical energy into work in a different way, burning fuel within an internal combustion process (Figure 2.7b). It may achieve up to 35-40% overall efficiency. Similarly an internal combustion Diesel engine may have an overall efficiency of some 40%.

A modern combined cycle gas turbine plant (a CCGT) combines an open gas turbine with a closed Rankine cycle and may achieve an overall efficiency $\eta_O = W/f(CV)$ of up to 60%.

We give more details of practical plant efficiencies in Chapter 3.

2.8 Combined Heat and Power

For an industrial or domestic site requiring both electrical work and useful heat it is logical to ask why the heat rejected from an electric power generation plant cannot be utilised for the latter, instead of burning precious fuel in a parallel special heating device. The answer is that the heat rejected (e.g., from a large steam power station) is at a relatively low temperature (usually near atmospheric), at which it cannot be employed usefully.

However, it may be possible to design a power plant so that the heat is rejected at a slightly higher temperature, at which it is useful, perhaps in heating an apartment block. This leads to a plant with a smaller thermal efficiency (less work is being abstracted because of the higher rejection temperature). But since both useful work and useful heat are being produced, a higher fraction of the bound energy in the fuel is being used. It is wrong to say that this combined heat and power plant (CHP) has a higher overall efficiency. It does have higher energy utilisation, since more of the fuel energy is used, but it has a lower overall efficiency. An energy utilisation factor (EUF) may then be introduced of the form

$$(EUF) = (\dot{W} + \dot{Q}_U)/\dot{f}(CV). \qquad [2.23]$$

CHP is an attractive option where there is a simultaneous demand for both work and heat and we discuss such plants further in Chapter 5.

References

1. Keenan, J. H., 1941, *Thermodynamics*, John Wiley, New York.
2. Gyftopoulos, E. P. and Beretta, G. P., 1991, *Thermodynamic foundations and applications*. Macmillan, New York.
3. Haywood, R. W., 1980, *Equilibrium thermodynamics*. Wiley, London.
4. Rogers, G. F. C., and Mayhew, Y., 1992, *Engineering thermodynamics, work and heat transfer*, Longman's Scientific Publications, London.
5. Moran M. J., and Shapiro, H. N., 2007, *Fundamentals of engineering thermodynamics,* John Wiley, New York.
6. Montgomery, S. R., 1966, *Second Law of Thermodynamics*, Pergamon Press, Oxford.

Chapter 3
Work (Power) Production—
Stationary Power Plants

3.1 Introduction

In our society, there are enormous demands for power (the rate at which useful work is supplied and utilised). One of the main demands is for electrical power, which is used in commerce, industry, and domestically; its production requires over 30% ($0.33P$) of the world's primary energy consumption (P). It is the main call by our society on fossil fuels, and it is met primarily from central power stations, which then transmit the electricity at high voltage along electrical grids to consumers. But the electrical work used is about $0.13P$; much of the balance is wasted as heat, but not all, as some combined heat and power schemes utilise part of that heat.

A second major demand is power for transport, which absorbs about 20% of world primary energy consumption (about $0.2P$). This may take the form of electrical power to drive trains and buses, with the electricity again being generated in central power stations (and transported by high-voltage grids), or in local smaller power stations. But there is a dominant demand for the production of direct local power to drive cars and heavy transport. Here the convenience of the transportability of liquid fuels is vitally important.

We discuss here a variety of stationary power plants, deferring the discussion of power plants for transport until a later chapter.

3.2 Steam Power Plants

3.2.1 The Basic Rankine Plant

Most electrical power is produced in large steam power plants of up to 1,400 megawatts (MW) and of 35–40% thermal efficiency; these operate on the Rankine cycle, and until recently, were mainly coal-fired.

Figure 3.1 shows a simplified diagram of this type of plant. Fuel (coal, oil, or gas) is fed to a main boiler, which raises steam from a clean water supply. The steam is fed to a steam turbine, in which its high pressure is used

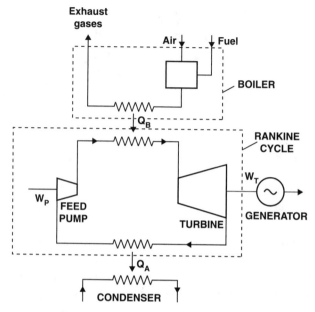

Fig. 3.1. Steam Power Plant with Rankine Closed Cycle

to produce steam at high velocity in stationary rows of turbine blades (stators). This steam drives round rotating disks carrying more turbine blades (rotors). There are many such stages in a steam turbine before the steam exhausts at low pressure into a condenser, where cooling water is used to condense the steam, which is then recirculated to the boiler. The rotating shaft of the turbine drives a generator delivering the electrical work.

The steam circuit is essentially closed (except for "make-up" water) and forms a cyclic heat engine, receiving heat from the boiler at a rate $\dot{Q}_B$ and rejecting heat in the condenser at a rate $\dot{Q}_A$. This is similar to the ideal steady flow Rankine heat engine of efficiency $(\eta_{CY})_{RANKINE}$ described in section 2.1.

The cycle efficiency of this practical plant η_{CY} is less than that of the ideal plant on which it is based $[(\eta_{CY})_{RANKINE}]$, because of imperfections or "irreversibilities." Its heat supply $(\dot{Q}_B)$ is generated within another control surface surrounding the boiler to which fuel is supplied at a rate $\dot{f}$. The "boiler" efficiency is

$$\eta_B = \dot{Q}_B / \dot{f}(CV) \qquad [3.1]$$

where (CV) is the calorific value of the fuel—its bound chemical energy per unit mass.

The overall efficiency of the practical plant is then

$$\eta_O = \dot{W}/\dot{f}(CV) = \eta_B \eta_{CY}. \qquad [3.2]$$

There is no simple expression for the efficiency of an ideal reversible Rankine steam cycle $(\eta_{CY})_{RANKINE}$; it is dependent primarily on the pressure and temperature of the steam supply and on the pressure in the condenser, which controls the temperature of heat rejection that is not far above atmospheric. Referring back to the ideal Carnot engine efficiency,

$$(\eta_{CY})_{CARNOT} = (T_B - T_A)/T_B, \qquad [3.3]$$

the Rankine cycle compares well thermodynamically in that all its heat rejection is at a low and constant temperature in the condenser. However, its heat supply is variable in temperature, only the final part is supplied at the maximum temperature of the steam, a temperature limited by that which the blading of the turbine can withstand.

3.2.2 Measures to Raise the Mean Temperature of Heat Supply

The mean temperature of supply increases with the pressure of the steam, but another important way in which the mean temperature of supply can be increased (and hence the cycle efficiency) is by reheating. After partial expansion of the steam through the turbine, it is extracted and heated again to a high temperature, with an additional external heat supply, before it is returned to the turbine for further expansion. Exceptionally, this process can be repeated in a second stage of reheating.

The mean temperature of heat supply can also be increased if the water temperature at entry to the boiler is increased above the condenser temperature. This can be achieved by "regenerative feed heating." A small quantity of steam is extracted from the turbine and used to raise the temperature of the water supply to the boiler, in an "internal" feed heater, which does not need any further external heat supply. As with reheating, this regenerative feed heating process can be repeated in other feed heaters, and the total fraction of steam extracted may be substantial, up to about 0.35 in some modern plants. The reader is referred to standard textbooks (e.g., Haywood [1]) for full details of these two important modifications of the basic Rankine cycle (reheating and regenerative feed heating).

The real steam plant is irreversible with several imperfections, which include heat and pressure losses round the cycle, and the turbine inlet temperature is limited by material considerations. The flow in the turbine itself is more or less adiabatic (only a small fraction of the heat supplied is lost there) but it is not ideal in thermodynamics terms. The irreversibility is mainly due to internal fluid friction in the steam flow through the turbine blading. Similarly, the boiler flow is not reversible, although the efficiency of a good power plant boiler may be high and attain some 90%.

3.2.3 Calculations of Practical Steam Plant Efficiency

Calculation of the real steam plant efficiency is a complex task and we do not tackle it here. Rather, we present the results of some typical calculations by Haywood (2) in which practical assumptions were made (e.g. for the losses in the steam flow through the turbine). The result of one set of these calculations is illustrated in Figure 3.2, for a cycle with double reheat and with a condenser temperature just above standard ambient. This figure shows the importance of two features, both of which raise the mean temperature of heat supply and hence the thermal efficiency:

a. increasing the pressure level at which the steam is raised in the boiler;

b. increasing the final feed water temperature (by regenerative feed heating).

The effect of changes in the maximum turbine inlet temperature (at a given boiler pressure) are not shown here. The turbine inlet temperature shown in the diagram is quite high for modern practice, but major efforts are now being made to increase that temperature even further, to 700°C and beyond, in order to raise plant efficiency. This requires developments in turbine materials. An old rule of thumb for steam turbine design engineers is that raising the turbine inlet temperature by 10°C leads to a gain in overall efficiency of 0.25%.

Modern steam plants may have the steam supply raised to very high pressure levels, even to what is described as super-critical level (above the critical pressure at which steam can be raised from water with no requirement for latent heat in evaporation at constant temperature). Such plants are complex and expensive and until recently have only been constructed in the developed countries. Steam plants in these countries generally have higher efficiencies than those in developing countries, and this is a factor in the distribution of primary energy used around the world.

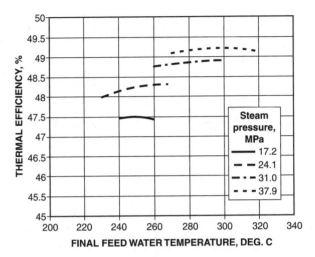

Fig. 3.2. Calculations of the Thermal Efficiencies of Practical Steam Plants, as a Function of Final Feed Water Temperature, with Various Steam Pressure Levels (MN/m²). Double Reheat Cycle with Maximum Steam Temperatures 649/593/593°C

Steam boilers for power plants are usually fired by coal, although oil and natural gas are also used to a lesser extent. Thus electricity generation leads to substantial discharge of carbon dioxide to the atmosphere, an important feature to which we shall return later in Chapter 7. Plants burning lignite (soft coal) have to dispose of substantial quantities of ash.

3.3 Gas Turbine Plants

3.3.1 The Open Gas Turbine Plant

The next most widely used plant for generating electricity is that based on the "open cycle" gas turbine. It is self contained in that it requires no external heater or boiler, fuel being supplied directly to an internal combustion chamber within the plant itself, rather than to an external heater as in a steam power plant.

Figure 3.3 shows a diagram of a simple open gas turbine plant. Air is drawn into a compressor, which compresses the air before it enters the combustion chamber, to which fuel (natural gas or light oil) is also fed. The high temperature products of combustion are supplied to a gas turbine, which has two functions—first, to drive the compressor, and second, to drive an elec-

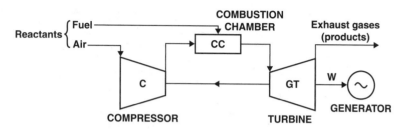

Fig. 3.3. Open Cycle Gas Turbine Plant

tric generator. The gases are then discharged to the atmosphere at exit from the turbine.

This open cycle gas turbine plant is not a heat engine in the strict thermodynamic sense as it uses internal combustion and there is an irreversible change in the combustion chamber from the reactants used, fuel and air, to combustion products. After flow through the turbine, these gases are not returned to the compressor entry to complete a cycle but are discharged to the atmosphere.

The overall efficiency of the practical open gas turbine power plant is

$$\eta_o = \dot{W}/\dot{f}(CV) \qquad\qquad [3.4]$$

where $\dot{W}$ is the net power delivered, $\dot{f}$ is the fuel flow rate, and (CV) is the calorific value.

In recent years, these simple gas turbine plants have become quite large, up to 300 MW, although this is still much less than a modern steam power plant. However, several gas turbines may be used in parallel in a large power station. Overall efficiencies over 40% can now be achieved.

3.3.2 The Closed Cycle Gas Turbine Plant and the Air Standard (Joule-Brayton) Cycle

Another type of power plant involving a gas turbine can operate on a *closed* cycle, usually, but not always, using air; the steam turbine of Figure 3.1 is now replaced by a gas turbine as illustrated in Figure 3.4. Air is now compressed in the compressor and then receives heat from a heater separately and externally fired with fuel. The high-pressure, high-temperature air then expands through the gas turbine, which drives both the compressor and an external electricity generator as in the open circuit plant of Figure 3.3. The air is then cooled before it is returned to the compressor entry, this completing the internal cycle.

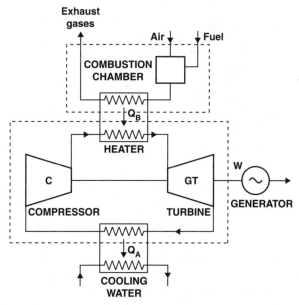

Fig. 3.4. Closed Circuit Gas Turbine Power Plant
with Joule-Brayton Cycle

This closed cycle plant can be simulated by an air standard steady flow cycle—the so-called Joule-Brayton constant pressure cycle. This is illustrated in Figure 3.5 on a pressure-specific volume diagram (volume per unit mass of air). Air at state 1 is compressed reversibly and adiabatically (without any heat transfer) to state 2; heat is then added at constant pressure at a rate $\dot{Q}_B$, between state 2 and state 3 (at which the temperature reaches a maximum); the air is then expanded reversibly and adiabatically to state 4; finally heat is then extracted at constant pressure at a rate $\dot{Q}_A$, between state 4 and the original state 1, the cycle thus being completed. The efficiency of this steady flow cyclic heat engine, in which air is assumed to be a perfect gas (with the values of gas constant R and specific heats c_p and c_v all constant), is simply

$$(\eta_{CY})_{JOULE} = \frac{\dot{W}}{\dot{Q}_B} = \frac{\dot{Q}_B - \dot{Q}_A}{\dot{Q}_B} \qquad [3.5]$$

The net power output $\dot{W}$ is the power delivered in full expansion less the power input required for compression; these processes are similar to those in a real closed cycle gas turbine plant, but in the air standard cycle they are assumed to be reversible and adiabatic (with no heat transfer). Thus, al-

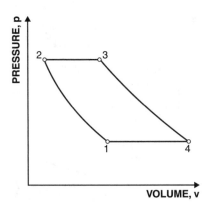

Figure 3.5 Joule-Brayton Cycle on a Pressure—
Specific Volume Diagram

though the operation of a real closed cycle gas turbine power plant is simulated by this Joule-Brayton air standard cycle, its efficiency is less than $(\eta_{CY})_{JOULE}$ because of frictional and other losses.

It is a straightforward matter to analyse the air standard Joule-Brayton cycle, see Haywood (1), determining its classical heat engine efficiency $(\eta_{CY})_{JOULE}$ as the power output divided by rate at which heat is supplied. $(\eta_{CY})_{JOULE}$ may be shown to be a function of a single performance parameter, the pressure ratio, $r_p = p_2/p_1$,

$$(\eta_{CY})_{JOULE} = f(r_p). \tag{3.6}$$

The temperatures levels do not appear directly, but they are present indirectly through the pressure ratio (1). This relation is plotted in Figure 3.6 and it is seen that efficiency increases markedly with the pressure ratio.

3.3.3 Calculations of Practical Gas Turbine Plant Efficiency

The thermal efficiency of practical gas turbine plants (both open and closed types) will be less than the efficiency of the Joule cycle because the real processes are not reversible. Further, material and mechanical considerations will impose limitations, particularly through the maximum temperature at turbine entry. Estimates of plant overall efficiency again involve complex calculations and are not undertaken here, but (η_o) is primarily dependent on two factors, not only the pressure ratio in the compressor (as to be expected from the Joule cycle) but now also the maximum turbine entry tem-

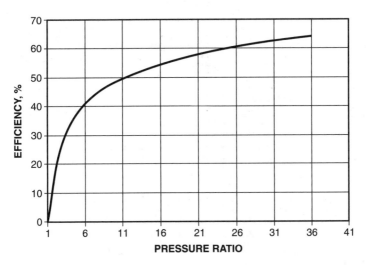

Figure 3.6 Cyclic Efficiency of the Joule-Brayton Cycle,
as a Function of Pressure Ratio

perature. To a lesser extent, the plant performance also depends on the efficiencies of the flows through the compressor and turbine (as in the steam turbine plant these are related primarily to the amount of the internal friction within the blading).

A set of calculations for an industrial type open circuit gas turbine plant, taken from Horlock (3), are shown in Figure 3.7; these do now illustrate the importance of the maximum turbine inlet temperature T_3, which depends on combustion in the open plant. (This feature would be expected from the earlier discussion in Chapter 2 of the ideal Carnot cycle plant.) The role of the pressure ratio is more indirect. An increase in pressure ratio for a given maximum (combustion) temperature generally increases the *mean* temperature of "heat supply" (the average temperature in the combustion or heating process) but lowers the *mean* temperature of "heat rejection."

3.3.4 Variations on the Simple Open Gas Turbine Plant

There are several variations on the simple open gas turbine plant (3), aimed at increasing thermal efficiency and/or the specific power output—the power per unit flow rate (1). As for the steam cycle, the mean temperature of heat supply can be raised by reheating, splitting the turbine expansion into two parts and reheating the gas between the two in a second combustion chamber. However, in the gas turbine plant this action does not

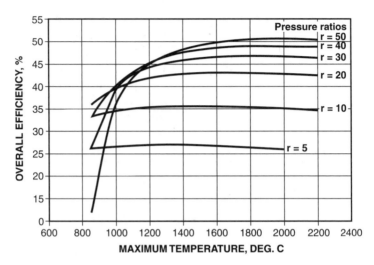

Fig. 3.7. Calculations of thr Thermal Efficiencies of Practical
Open Circuit Gas Turbine Plants as a Function of Maximum
(Combustion) Temperature and Various Pressure Ratios

generally increase the efficiency—only the specific power output (the work output per unit of mass flow circulating).

Another variation involves intercooling, splitting the compression process in two, cooling the air and then returning it to the second stage of compression. This lowers the mean temperature of heat rejection and its effect is similar to reheating in that it increases the specific power of the plant but generally not its efficiency. However, introducing *both* reheating and intercooling does raise overall efficiency, since it takes the plant towards a Carnot cycle.

More importantly the maximum temperature of the gas at turbine entry can be increased if the turbine blade material is cooled. Thus, an important feature of modern open cycle gas turbines is "turbine cooling," in which some of the compressed air is bypassed around the combustion chamber and used to cool the turbine blades, down to a temperature that the material can withstand. Turbine cooling then enables higher combustion temperatures to be used but involves some irreversible processes which involve loss of plant efficiency. Generally there is a gain in performance from turbine cooling, which enables the combustion temperature to be increased, but there may be a thermodynamic limit on this action because the cooling flows become too great. This is illustrated in the calculations shown in Figure 3.7.

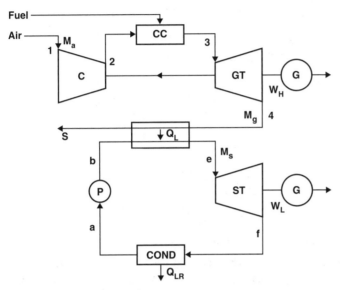

Fig. 3.8. The Combined Cycle Gas Turbine Plant

3.4 Combined Cycle Gas Turbine Plants (CCGTs)

One recently developed plant has gained a substantial share of electricity generation, the combined cycle gas turbine or CCGT. It combines an open cycle (combustion) gas turbine with a steam turbine plant, and is illustrated simply in Figure 3.8.

The gas turbine drives a generator as in the normal combustion turbine plant, but its exhaust, still at quite high temperature, is then used to supply a waste heat boiler (or heat recovery steam generator, HRSG) in a "bottoming" Rankine cycle with a steam turbine driving its own electricity generator. Thus the waste heat in the gas turbine exhaust is used to give more power and this increases the thermal efficiency from some 35–40% in the simple gas turbine plant to about 55% or even higher in the CCGT.

These plants have gained great popularity with the increased availability of natural gas as a fuel in recent years. Again there are a number of variations on the basic CCGT plant leading to even higher thermal efficiency and the reader is referred to other texts for details (e.g., Horlock [3]). Some CCGT plants are used in a combined heat and power (CHP) form (see Chapter 5).

A plot of combined cycle efficiency against the basic design parameters (i.e., against combustion temperature and pressure ratio in the gas turbine,

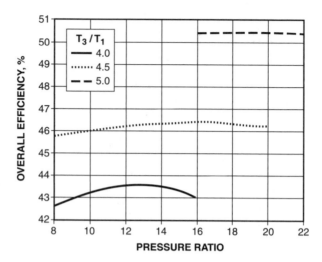

Fig. 3.9. Calculations of the Thermal Efficiencies of Practical CCGT Plants as a Function of Pressure Ratio and for Various Values of the Ratio of Maximum (Combustion) Temperature T_3 to Atmospheric Temperature T_1 (Single Pressure Steam Cycle)

but with constant maximum turbine inlet temperature and condensing temperature in the steam turbine cycle) is shown in Figure 3.9. The overall plant efficiency may approach the Carnot efficiency for the same maximum and minimum temperatures, so there is not a great deal more that the engineer can deliver from the primary energy in the fuel. Thermodynamics is beginning to set the limit on overall plant performance.

3.5 Integrated Gasification Combined Cycle Plants (IGCC)

An important modification of the CCGT plant involves using coal as a fuel rather than natural gas, the integrated gasification combined cycle plant (IGCC). This not only enables an alternative, widely available fuel to be used, but it can be modified to separate carbon dioxide, for liquefaction and storage (carbon sequestration and storage [CSS]). This is likely to be a very important plant in future as we shall see in the later chapter on pollution and global warming.

3.5.1 The Basic IGCC Plant

An IGCC plant is illustrated in simplified form in Figure 3.10. Coal is ground and mixed with water to form a slurry, and this is fed to the gasifier

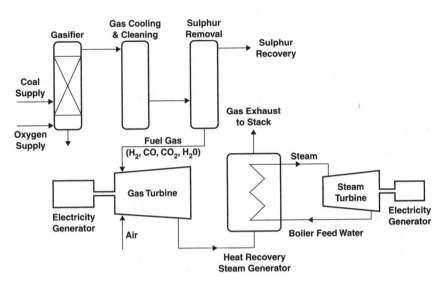

Fig. 3.10. The Basic IGCC Plant

through a burner in which partial combustion takes place with oxygen (supplied from a separate plant). During gasification the coal ash is melted into a slag, quenched with water and removed as a solid. Following the high temperature reactions of the coal and water with the oxygen, raw synthetic gas (syngas), consisting mainly of hydrogen and carbon monoxide (about 40% each by molal concentration), is water-cooled in radiant and convection coolers, generating saturated steam. The gas is then passed through a particulate scrubber, further cooled to near ambient temperature prior to sulphur removal.

The syngas then enters the conventional exhaust heated CCGT plant, being burnt in the gas turbine combustion chamber with air from the compressor. The combustion gas supplies the gas turbine, driving the compressor and a generator, and then exhausts into the HRSG (unfired), which raises superheated steam. By-product steam from the gasifier coolers (some 40% of the total steam supply) can also be superheated in the HRSG and supplied to the steam turbine, which drives its own generator.

3.5.2 Modification of the Basic IGCC Plant

The basic IGCC plant can be modified by adding a further reaction step that converts the carbon monoxide into carbon dioxide, with the production of more hydrogen downstream of the gasifier. Figure 3.11 illustrates a plant

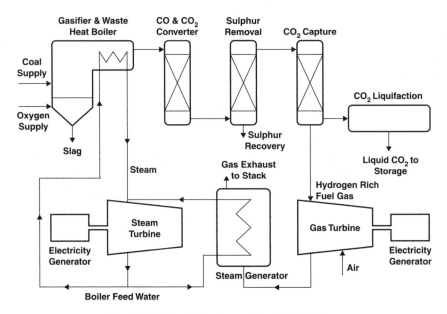

Fig. 3.11. Modification of the IGCC Plant
to Extract Carbine Dioxide

involving this type of modification. It also shows a method of recovering the carbon dioxide by absorption at high pressure and recovery by liquefaction. The plant is called an IGCC/CSS plant, for carbon sequestration and storage.

3.6 Internal Combustion Engines (IC)

There are smaller power plants generating electricity, which are based on reciprocating internal combustion engines (particularly those burning gas or fuel oil), but they do not deliver a large proportion of electricity worldwide. They may be used in central power stations primarily as standby plants, but there is wider use of small units in industry and large commercial buildings, particularly in combined heat and power form. We discuss such IC engine power plants in Chapter 6 on work (and power) for transport, where their use is dominant.

3.7 Nuclear Plants

The heat generator in a nuclear power plant is the nuclear reactor in which fission of a radioactive fuel such as uranium takes place. In nuclear fission a neutron is absorbed by the nucleus of a uranium-235 atom, which in turn splits into fast-moving lighter elements (fission products) and free neutrons, and other nuclear fragments such as beta particles and alpha particles, together with gamma rays.

Fission of heavy elements is an exothermic reaction and can release substantial amounts of useful energy. It is thus useful as a heat source because some materials both generate neutrons as part of the fission process and also undergo successive fissions when impacted by a free neutron. In thermal reactors, the commonest form of power plant reactor, the neutrons resulting from a fission are slowed down by a moderator (graphite or pressurised water) before they move on to the next fission in a chain reaction. Thus nuclear fuels can be part of a self-sustaining chain reaction that releases energy at a controlled rate in a nuclear reactor.

The amount of bound energy contained in a nuclear fuel is many times the amount of bound energy contained in a similar mass of chemical fuel. However, the waste products of nuclear fission are highly radioactive and remain so for many years, presenting a problem of disposal of nuclear waste problem.

The reactor cores can be cooled by gas (carbon dioxide in the early U.K. nuclear plants), or by pressurised water, as in most American, French, and Russian plants. The gas or water heated in this way is then used to raise steam in a secondary heater, essentially acting as the boiler in a Rankine cycle (see Figure 3.12 for a simplified circuit diagram of a gas-cooled plant). Alternatively the reactor may supply heat to a closed-circuit gas turbine power plant.

The overall efficiency of a nuclear power plant is not as high as that of a high-pressure conventional steam power plant, or a modern CCGT plant; however this is less critical since the reserves of nuclear fuel are very large indeed. Further, unlike fossil fuels, they produce virtually no carbon dioxide.

Some reactors can be used not only as power reactors but also to produce more radioactive material; these are called fast breeder reactors. A fast reactor is a category of reactor in which the fission chain reaction is continued by fast neutrons. Such a reactor needs no neutron moderator to slow the neutrons down to thermal levels of energy but it must use fuel that is relatively rich in fissile material compared to that required for a thermal reactor. Absorption in the moderator is a major loss of neutrons in a thermal reactor, so a fast reactor has a much better neutron economy; there is a much larger excess of neutrons not required to sustain the chain reaction. Indeed a fast reactor can produce enough neutrons to enable it to breed more fuel

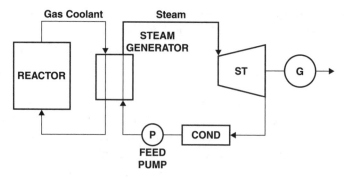

Fig. 3.12. Simplified Diagram of a Gas-cooled Nuclear Power Plant

than it consumes. Production of fissile material takes place to some extent in the fuel of all nuclear power reactors but to be called a breeder, a reactor must be specifically designed to create more fissile material than it consumes.

A breeder reactor consumes fissile material at the same time as it creates new fissile material. This occurs by neutron irradiation of fertile material, particularly uranium-238 and thorium-232. These materials are provided, either in the fuel or in a breeder blanket surrounding the core, or both. Fast breeder reactors will be of vital importance in world energy developments, although they do not contribute a substantial fraction of electricity generation at present.

An ambitious development of nuclear plants will involve not the fission of heavy elements but fusion of light atoms to form heavier ones, leading to the release of very large amounts of energy. This fusion process requires very high temperatures before it can take place. Scientific work to achieve fusion is proceeding but the engineering of a fusion power plant will involve major development. There are no fusion power plants operational at present; indeed such plants are many years away, and are unlikely to solve the world's energy problems in the first half of the twenty-first century.

3.8 Fuel Cells

An attractive small power plant is the fuel cell, an electrochemical device in which the chemical energy of the fuel is converted directly into electricity. It has high efficiency, unlimited by the Second Law. A phosphoric acid fuel cell is illustrated in Figure 3.13. Hydrogen and carbon dioxide are fed to an anode located within the phosphoric acid electrolyte. Hydrogen ions flow to the cathode, which is fed with air. Electrons flow in the counter direction to

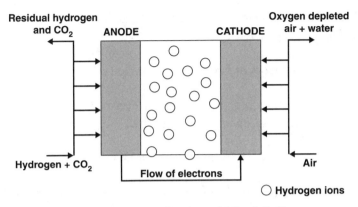

Fig. 3.13. Phosphoric Acid Fuel Cell

the hydrogen ions, through an external circuit, providing the generated electricity. Residual hydrogen and carbon dioxide are discharged from the anode, and oxygen-depleted air and water leave the cathode.

Although the principle has been known for over 250 years, the fuel cell has not been competitive as an electricity generator. Other types of fuel cell are based on different electrolytes—molten carbonate, solid oxide and solid polymer.

In general, fuel cells, although potentially highly efficient, are of low voltage and have to be stacked to produce significant power output. Current efficiencies range from 30 to 60%, but they are capital expensive, which drives up the price of the electricity they generate. However, costs will come down with improved technology and substantial production. They will also become more attractive, particularly for transport, as gas and oil supplies become scarcer.

3.9 Renewable Power Plants

There are other power plants used to generate electricity which do not use either fossil fuels or uranium—so-called renewable plants. The major renewable plants are large hydro plants using gravitational flow of water to drive water turbines. The next most important renewable generators involve wind power; others include wave, tidal, and solar power plants. In 2005, such plants contributed electrical work equivalent to that which could have been supplied by conventional power plants equal to some 5% of the world's demand for primary energy.

We shall not describe these renewable generation plants here but defer more detailed discussion to Chapter 8, after discussion of pollution and global warming in Chapter 7.

3.10 The Financial Cost of Producing Electricity

It is shown in Appendix A that P_E, the annual cost of electricity produced (e.g., $ per annum), is given approximately by

$$P_E = \beta C_0 + M + (OM) \qquad [3.6]$$

where C_0 is the capital cost of plant (e.g., $); β (i,N) is a capital charge factor, which is related to the discount rate (i) on capital and the life of the plant $(N$ years) M is the annual cost of fuel supplied (e.g., $ p.a.); (OM) is the annual cost of operation and maintenance (e.g., $ p.a.).

The unitised production cost Y_E (in say $ per kilowatt hour) for the plant is then written as

$$(Y_E) = \frac{P_E}{\dot{W}H} = \frac{\beta C_0}{\dot{W}H} + \frac{M}{\dot{W}H} + \frac{(OM)}{\dot{W}H}, \qquad [3.7]$$

which can be developed (see Appendix A) to give

$$(Y_E) = \frac{\beta C_0}{\dot{W}H} + \frac{S}{(CV)_0 (\eta)_0} + \frac{(OM)}{\dot{W}H}, \qquad [3.8]$$

where $\dot{W}$ is the rating of the plant (kW), H is the plant utilisation (hours per annum), S is the cost of fuel per unit mass (say $/kg), $(CV)_0$ is the calorific value (kWh/kg), and $(\eta_0) = \dfrac{\dot{W}}{\dot{f}(CV)_0}$ is the overall efficiency of the plant,

delivering power $\dot{W}$ from a fuel energy supply rate $\dot{f}$.

Figure 3.14 shows simply how $(P_E/\dot{W}H)$, less the $(OM/\dot{W}H)$ component, varies with the capital cost factor and the "heat rate" in kJ/kWh (which is proportional to the inverse of the overall efficiency η_0), for $H = 4,000$ hours and $\zeta = S/(CV)_0 = 1$ c/kWh. Horlock (3) has used this type of chart to compare three lines of development in gas turbine power generation:

    a.   a heavy-duty simple cycle gas turbine, of moderate capital cost, with a relatively low pressure ratio and modest thermal efficiency (36%);

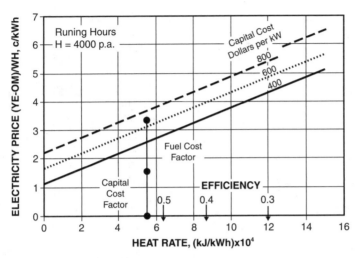

Fig. 3.14. Unit Cost of Electricity—Effect of (*a*) Capital Cost Factor and (*b*) Fuel Cost Factor (Plant Efficiency) for Given Plant Utilization

    b.   an aero-engine derivative simple cycle gas turbine, usually two-shaft and of high pressure ratio, the capital cost per kilowatt of this plant being surprisingly little different from (*a*) in spite of its being derived from developed aero-engines, with thermal efficiency slightly higher (39%);

    c.   a heavy-duty CCGT plant, based on (*a*), which has a high thermal efficiency but increased capital cost.

Rough locations for types (*a*), (*b*), and (*c*) are given on the electricity price charts of Figures 3.15 and 3.16, for 8,000 hours and 4,000 hours utilisation, respectively. For 8,000 hours, the CCGT plant type (*c*) has a clear advantage in spite of increased capital costs. At 4,000 hours the CCGT plant loses this advantage over the aero-engine derivatives because of the increase in the capital cost element (*H* has been decreased).

    However, more direct comparisons should include factors of operational and maintenance, the cost of which have been omitted in the presentations of Figures. 3.15 and 3.16 on the following page.

References

1.   Haywood, R. W., 1991, *Analysis of Engineering Cycles*, 4th ed., Per-gamon Press, Oxford.

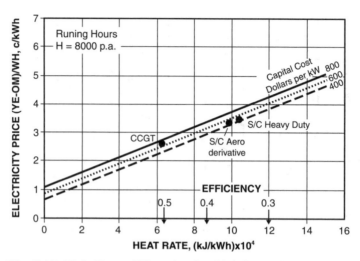

Fig. 3.15. Unit Cost of Electricy for Simple Cycle and CCGT Plants for High Utilization Factor

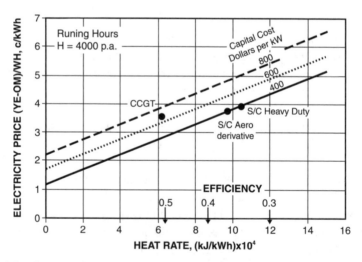

Fig. 3.16. Unit Cost of Electricy for Simple Cycle and CCGT Plants for Low Utilization

2. Haywood, R. W., 1957 *Steam Cycle calculations for Supercritical Pressures*, Unpublished C.E.G.B. Report.
3. Horlock, J. H. 2005, *Advanced Gas Turbine Cycles*, Pergamon, Oxford.

Chapter 4
Heating and Refrigeration Processes

4.1 Introduction

We have described some of the many different means of producing power from stationary power plants. We now discuss various ways in which much of the world's primary energy supply (*P*), mainly bound chemical energy, is converted into *heat*. We defer until Chapter 8 a discussion of heating using renewable sources, but we do describe here how energy is used in producing cold (refrigeration schemes).

We stated in Chapter 1 that about a third of the world's primary energy (0.33*P*) is used in generating electrical work of about 0.13*P*, noting that most of the remaining difference goes into waste heat rejected from the power plants, although some is converted into useful heat in combined heat and power (CHP) plants. There are other energy losses of transformation before energy becomes useful heat and work.

Hills, in chapter 9 of (1), suggests that 20% of the world's primary energy goes into producing power for transport, but the International Energy Agency (IEA) data (2) suggests this is an overestimate (here we take 0.17*P*). We discuss that transfer of energy later, but again note that well over half of this also goes into rejected heat eventually, usually in the form of exhaust gases from the portable power plants.

IEA data (2) shows other uses as summarised in Table 4.1. There is some overlap in this table—for example, of the 0.17*P* for industry about a quarter is use of electricity, and the rest is in the form of heating—so the items in the table do not sum to *P*. Of the 0.17*P* for residential about 7% is electrical and of the 0.05*P* for commercial about 50% is electrical. Of the traditional renewable biomass sources (i.e., wood, agricultural waste, etc.), about 0.1*P* is used in the developing countries, mainly for heating rather than for power.

This very approximate exercise emphasises the substantial amount of energy that is used for heating in industry and commercial and domestic buildings, and we discuss these aspects now.

53

**Table 4.1 Approximate Breakdown of World's
Primary Energy Use (P)**

Electricity Generation	0.33P (producing 0.13P electrical work)
Transport	0.17P
Industrial	0.17P
Residential	0.17P
Commercial and public services	0.05P
Traditional fuels, mainly used for heating	0.1P

4.2 Types of Heaters

As has been indicated earlier, most of the primary energy the world uses is supplied by fossil fuels (see Figure 4.1). Most of this primary energy, perhaps 70%, is used in combustion within a range of heating devices—boilers for stationary power plants, furnaces or kilns, and fires—many using coal. Most of the remaining percentage of primary energy used goes into internal combustion engines producing power directly and using gas and oil.

Heating devices may be classified either by the purpose for which they are used, in power plants, in industrial processes, in commercial and domestic heating of buildings, or by the basis of the fuel they use such as coal, gas, oil, etc. Here we adopt the first classification, but also refer to the fuels that may be used in the various applications.

4.2.1 Heaters in Power Plants

Heaters which are coupled to cyclic steam power plants (e.g., coal-fired boilers linked to Rankine-type steam plants), use a variety of fuels, mainly coal, gas, and oil, and to a lesser extent energy crops, waste (industrial and municipal), and landfill gas. The performance of these boilers is vitally important as the first stage in the production of power, their direct function being to supply heat to the closed power cycle itself.

Nuclear reactors are similarly external boilers for cyclic steam plants (see Chapter 3). We do not discuss here the combustion processes within power plants such as open-cycle gas turbines and reciprocating internal combustion engines.

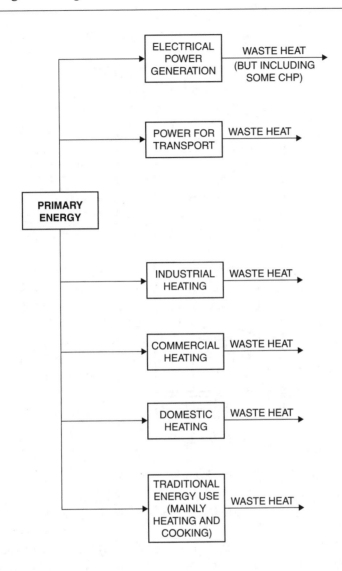

Fig. 4.1. Energy Flows for Heating (see Table 4.1)

Coal is still the dominant fuel in boilers for steam power plants. The essential parts of a steam boiler are shown in Figure 4.2. The products of combustion supply heat first to water from the Rankine cycle condenser, which is pumped up to boiler pressure. This water is raised to evaporation temperature in an economiser placed in the boiler flue gases, as illustrated

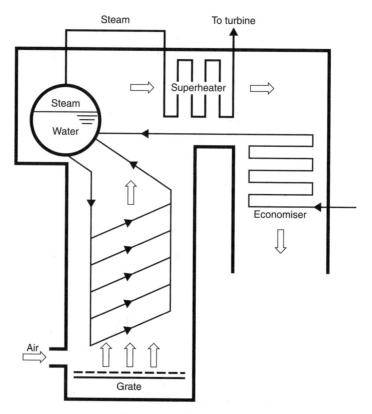

Fig. 4.2. Boiler

in the figure. It is then heated by the combustion products in a complex arrangement of boiler tubes, some on the walls of the boiler. In the "water-wall" riser tubes, the steam is generated and the resulting steam-water mixture is discharged to a steam drum, the unevaporated water returning through "down-comer" pipes to the feet of the water walls by a process of natural circulation. Saturated steam drawn off from the steam drum is then finally heated by the flue gases in a superheater, which raises the steam temperature at approximately constant pressure to its final superheated state. Together with the low temperature economiser, this superheating process ensures that further energy is recovered from the flue gases before they are discharged to the atmosphere. (Preheating of the air before combustion may also be used to extract energy from the flue gases, reducing the amount of fuel used in the cycle and raising the boiler efficiency.)

Condensation of the flue gases on the outside of economiser tubes may prove a hazard, particularly if the original fuel contains sulphur, so the vapour within the flue gases may condense at a higher temperature causing corrosion of the economiser tubes.[1] It should be noted that if regenerative feed heating is used in the Rankine cycle, increasing water temperatures (see Chapter 3), there may be no need for an economiser.

There are three main types of coal-fired boiler:

1. *Grate* boilers in which coal, in relatively small pieces, is fed in from a hopper or conveyor belt, moving across the grate through which air flows;
2. *Pulverised coal* (PC) boilers in which small particles of coal are swept in by an air flow to the burner jets;
3. *Fluidised bed combustion* (FBC) boilers, usually atmospheric (AFBC), in which coal and limestone form a bed through which air is blown, forming "bubbles" for "bubbling fluidised bed combustion."

Development of the last process has led to circulating fluidised beds (CFBC), the partially combusted gases and solids recycling through the bed, and to pressurised fluidised beds (PFBC) where the pressure may be increased to many times the atmospheric pressure.

A good description of power plant boilers is given in the main Open University course book on energy systems (3). More advanced discussions on the comparative merits of various modern types of boiler are given by Pillai and a broad picture on utilisation of both PC and FBC boilers is supplied by Preston, both in Rooke et al. (1).

4.2.2 Industrial Heating Processses

Heating processes in industry may conveniently be divided into low and high temperature (less than and greater than 200°C, respectively). A small but important proportion of the primary energy used is for the *low-temperature heating processes* (at less than 200°C). Most of these low-temperature processes involve some metals manufacture, ceramics, and miner-

---

[1] In domestic condensing boilers (really water heaters rather than boilers raising steam), economisers may be used to extract flue gas energy and raise the circulating water temperature. Condensation of water vapour from the flue gases on the stainless steel tubes reduces the total energy discharged to the atmosphere and raises boiler efficiency; the condensed water is discharged separately.

als; others involve liquid heating and distillation. Such process heating is usually done by centrally generated steam from boilers, but some by CHP plants (see Chapter 5), and some by direct firing. A small part of the primary energy used goes into producing power from stationary plants, electrical power for pumps and fans, and for heating in the production processes themselves.

Masters, in chapter 8 of (1), gives a number of ways in which the primary energy used may be reduced in low-temperature heating processes.

    a. Process integration and intensification—optimum configuration of the overall process so that the various process streams may exchange heat with each other to provide heating and cooling rather than using external heating and cooling media.

    b. CHP plants yielding useful heat as well as electrical power.

    c. Heat pumps (see section 4.3.1).

High-temperature heating processes (at temperatures over 200°C) use about twice as much primary energy as the low-temperature processes, the iron and steel sectors being the largest users. Here direct firing is the major heating method, coke being the fuel most used, with gas and oil not far behind. But again some of the primary energy used goes to electrical power. These high-temperature processes (which may involve flame temperatures of above 1,900°C and material temperatures up to 1,600°C) are many and varied, but usually involve a refractory-lined kiln or furnace into which material is placed or transported.

Masters (1) also discusses ways in which the primary energy used in these high temperature processes may be reduced.

    a. Heat recovery from the flue gases into the product stream. Here the approach is essentially to define a furnace or a kiln as a "counter flow" heat exchanger in which the combustion flue gases form the hot stream and the products (e.g., steel billets) form the cold stream.

    b. Heat recovery from the flue gases into the combustion air (and possibly gaseous fuel), which may also be achieved as in a contraflow heat exchanger. Alternatively, in regenerative transient systems, the flue gases are first blown into a massive chequerwork of bricks for up to thirty minutes when the cold airflow is reversed and enters the hot chequerwork for preheating prior to combustion.

    c. Other ways of reducing the primary energy include the use of mod-

ern furnace materials such as lightweight ceramic fibre furnace lin-
ings, oxygen enriched combustion air, and advanced control systems.

These various methods have led to substantial increases in furnace efficiency
(defined in the same way as boiler efficiency).

4.2.3 Heating in the Commercial Sector

In the developed countries, a substantial amount of primary energy goes
into heating buildings in the commercial sectors (offices, retail, health care,
education, leisure and hotels). Heating is mainly by fossil-fired boilers (usually providing hot water), but some is by electric heating. CHP plants are
increasingly used, which meet the power demands as well as the heat requirements. Boilers usually have efficiencies in the 65–80% range; CHP
plants may have low-thermal efficiencies, of 30% or less, but supply perhaps an additional 50% of their primary energy in heat, giving an overall
energy utilisation factor (*EUF*) of 80%. This can be economically attractive
in a large supermarket or a hospital. There are some instances (e.g., greenhouses) where the low-temperature heat from conventional power stations is
used directly. There has been increasing demand for electrical power in commercial buildings in recent years, for office equipment, computers, and air
conditioning, leading to increased consumption of primary fossil fuel energy.
Industrial buildings such as factories or warehouses have heating devices similar to those in commercial buildings. However, there may not always be a need for continuous heating, or heating the whole building, so
local heaters (often electrical) may be used.

4.2.4 Domestic Heating

The majority of homes in the developed countries are now heated by
central heating systems, using hot water boilers, although a substantial fraction use electrical space heating. Condensing boilers of higher efficiency
have been increasingly used in recent years (see later), and some houses
now use heat pumps (see also later). In very cold countries such as Sweden,
Denmark, and Russia, large CHP schemes have been introduced for blocks
of flats. These have to be designed for both winter (space heating, hot water,
and power demands) and summer (usually power and hot water demands
only) but can prove economic if on a large scale.

4.3 Novel Heating Systems

There are several other less-standard heating systems coming into use that offer opportunities for saving primary energy.

4.3.1 Heat Pumps

Another nominally attractive heating system is the heat pump (see Figure 4.3a), which operates on the same principles as a refrigerator, Figure 4.3b (fuller details of the thermodynamic cycle are given in section 4.5). With the help of a work input, the heat pump takes heat from a low-temperature source and delivers much more heat to a higher temperature (see Figure 4.3a). However, the temperature levels are different from those in most refrigeration systems. The heat is usually taken from the surrounding environment, such as a river or the surrounding ground, at a low ambient temperature, and delivered to a house or commercial building at a comfortable living temperature. How well the heat pump performs is usually measured by a coefficient of performance, the ratio of the useful heat delivered (Q_U) to the work input required (W),

$$(CP)_{HP} = Q_U/W. \qquad [4.1]$$

The $(CP)_{HP}$ is a function of the temperature levels of operation, and for those heat pumps of interest in domestic or commercial application may be of the order of 3.0 or even a little higher. A famous heat pump installed in Norwich during the second world war achieved an average performance of $(CP)_{HP} = 3.45$.

While apparently attractive to a consumer anxious to save on heating costs, the increased costs of electricity make the heat pump less economic in application. From the point of view of saving primary energy and reducing carbon dioxide production it may be attractive, but the useful heat provided is not for free. A unit of electrical input to a heat pump producing three units of useful heat still requires a primary energy input at the power station, of perhaps two and a half times that amount. Once again we are up against the second law, which requires us to provide a work input if we are to pump heat from a lower to a higher temperature. However, heat pumps with the work input supplied by from internal combustion engines (gas or liquid fuel fired), or even better by the work output from a CHP plant, can prove to be more attractive economically.

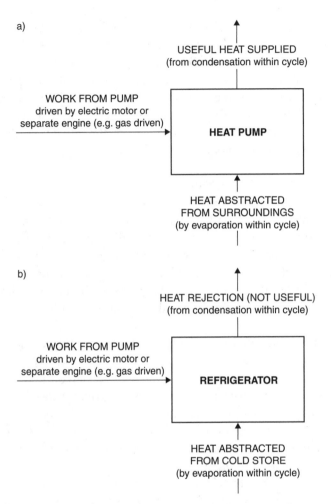

Fig. 4.3. *a*, Heat Pump, and *b*, Refrigerator

4.3.2 Condensing Boilers

A condensing boiler is a high-efficiency modern water heater that incorporates either a second heat exchanger or a larger main heat exchanger. It produces lower flue gas temperatures, lower flue gas emissions, and reduces fuel consumption. By recovering and using heat that would otherwise be lost up the flue, the very best high-efficiency boilers can operate with seasonal efficiencies of the order of 90%, compared to, typically, 75% for conventional types.

Recovering the heat from the flue reduces the temperature of the flue gases to a point where water vapour produced during combustion is condensed out. Thus the name high-efficiency condensing boiler. The heat recovered in this way is recirculated to preheat the water before it enters the main heat exchanger. (A side effect is that the condensed out water, known as condensate, which is sometimes acidic, has to be piped away to a drain or soakaway.) Although such high-efficiency boilers require a higher initial investment, they are very economical, and repay the extra initial cost in fuel savings in three or four years.

4.3.3 Renewable Heating Systems

Renewable heating usually utilises heat directly from the sun and may be passive (with no intervention) or active. We discuss these systems in Chapter 8 within the general discussion of renewables. Equally important in the search for reductions in the use of primary fuel and in carbon production is the elimination of heat losses, by better insulation etc. This important aspect of overall energy efficiency is also discussed later in Chapter 9.

4.4 Other Components Involving Heat Transfer or Rejection

There are many other processes involving the rejection or transfer of heat, which do not in themselves involve any input of primary energy.

In the Rankine cycle, an important component is the *condenser* (Figure 4.4). This receives wet steam, a mixture of steam vapour and water droplets, from the low-pressure turbine. Heat is transferred from this wet steam to cold water circulating through tubes on which the steam is condensed. It then flows to a pump, which increases the water pressure up to boiler pressure, sometimes in a staged process. The cooling water thus acts as a heat sink for the water/steam closed Rankine cycle.

There are many components involving heat transfer, particularly in chemical process plants, where heat is transferred in heat exchangers, from one hot stream to a colder one, as mentioned earlier in section 4.2.2. The science of heat transfer, which is also important in boiler and furnace design, is complex and not covered here. The author is referred to the standard texts (e.g., Rogers and Mayhew [4] for detailed discussion).

4.5 Refrigeration and Air Conditioning

The world's requirements for heat have been discussed, but there is a parallel requirement for cold, which is supplied in refrigeration plants, and these require a primary energy input (Figure 4.3b).

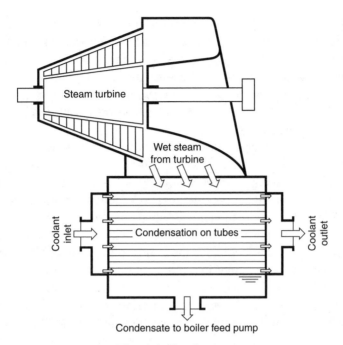

Fig. 4.4. Condenser

Large refrigerators for industrial or commercial application usually operate on a "reversed" vapour compression cycle. A liquid refrigerant, such as ammonia, is evaporated at low temperature and pressure, taking heat from its surroundings, the refrigeration effect. It is then compressed to a higher pressure and condensed at that higher temperature, yielding heat to the surroundings. Finally, the refrigerant is throttled back to the lower pressure to complete the cycle. The compression process requires an energy input, usually electrical, to drive a pump.

The performance of a refrigerator is measured by calculating the ratio of the heat it abstracts to the work input, the "coefficient of performance,"

$$(CP)_R = Q_{cold}/W_{in}.$$ [4.2]

Note that the CP for a refigerator involves the heat abstracted rather than the heat delivered as is the case for the heat pump. Thus,

$$(CP)_R = Q_{cold}/W_{in} = (Q_U - W)_{in}/W_{in} = (CP)_{HP} - 1.$$ [4.3]

Both coefficients of performance are strongly dependent on the two temperature levels at which the plants operate; and for a refrigerator the temperature differences between evaporation and condensation will be greater than those in a heat pump so that $(CP)_R$ may be of the order of 4, higher than $(CP)_{HP}$ for a heat pump despite the algebraic statement above. As far as the primary energy use is concerned, however, it has to be remembered that the power station producing the electricity requires perhaps three times the electrical work, so that the ratio of cold to primary energy used *(E)* is Q_{cold}/E and is then approximately 4/3.

Domestic refrigerators often operate on an absorption cycle in which the work of compression in the vapour compression cycle is reduced considerably by dissolving the refrigerant vapour in a suitable liquid before compression. At the higher pressure, heat is supplied to remove the vapour from solution. The refrigeration process then proceeds as in the vapour compression cycle (through condensation, throttling, and evaporation of the refrigerant). The work to compress the carrying liquid is less than that required to compress the vapour in a vapour compression cycle.

In an ingenious development of the absorption cycle, even the pump for compression is eliminated. The operation of the refrigerator now depends on the principle that if a liquid is exposed to an inert atmosphere, which is not saturated with the vapour of the refrigerant liquid, ammonia for example, some will evaporate. The partial pressure of the ammonia varies throughout the cycle being high in the condenser and low in the evaporator. This variation is achieved by concentration of a gas (such as hydrogen) in the parts of the circuit where the ammonia vapour pressure is low. Circulation of the refrigerant is achieved by convection currents set up by density gradients. (This cycle is usually called the Electrolux refrigeration cycle after the original industrial developers.) For these domestic refrigerators the definition of coefficient of performance becomes somewhat meaningless since the work input becomes so small or even zero.

A further requirement for energy input arises in the use of air conditioning in hot climates. Again the electricity input to an air conditioner must be produced in power plants where the primary energy is some three times that electrical work. Some years ago, an electrical blackout in the United States occurred in a hot summer when there was a very large demand for air conditioning, causing an overload on the electricity grid.

4.6 Discussion

This brief description of energy demand for heating illustrates some of the complexity of how a developed country uses primary energy. While there are great possibilities for energy savings in this whole area, such savings must depend on a variety of actions and methods, and while primary energy has been cheap, it has often been uneconomic until recently. The economic incentive to make savings in energy costs has not been dominant. However, with the cost of fuel increasing greatly, particularly gas and oil, the picture has changed. Further, the prospect of reducing carbon dioxide discharge and global warming, with governments offering tax incentives and subsidies, has emphasised the importance of savings in use of primary energy.

There are great possibilities for saving energy both by increasing the efficiency of the various heating methods and reducing the heat losses from the buildings and processes they serve. These two parallel actions fall within a broader discussion of increasing so-called energy efficiency in Chapter 9.

References

1. Rooke, D., Fells, I., and Horlock, J. H. [ed.], 1995, *Energy for the future*, Chapman and Hall, London.
2. Key World Energy Statistics, 2006, International Energy Agency, Paris.
3. Boyle, G. [ed.], 2003, *Energy systems and sustainability,* Oxford University Press, Oxford.
4. Rogers, G. F. C., and Mayhew, Y., 1992, *Engineering thermodynamics, work and heat transfer*, Longman's Scientific Publications, London.

Chapter 5
Combined Heat and Power (Cogeneration)

5.1 Introduction

As mentioned in Chapter 2, the combined heat and power (CHP) plant (sometimes called a cogeneration plant) appears to offer an attractive solution to a simultaneous demand for both heat and power. However, it is rare that a demand for both are maintained at more or less constant levels throughout the year. For example, a factory site may have a reasonably constant demand for power throughout the year but it will have a large demand for heat in winter (both space heating and hot water) but much less in the summer (probably hot water only). The ratio of heat to work demands (λ_D) is an important design parameter for CHP plants.

Demand usually varies greatly throughout the year (indeed, it may vary throughout the day), and the design of a CHP plant to match these requirements is a complex matter. It may be best to design the plant for the winter conditions and then waste some of the heat rejection in the summer, or it may be convenient to design for summer conditions and supplement the heat supply with a separate boiler in winter.

Because of these complications, it can be difficult to analyse the economics of a CHP plant replacing conventional plants (e.g., a power plant producing electricity only and a boiler producing useful heat). We referred in Chapter 3 to methods of calculating the price of electricity and give details in Appendix A. Later in this chapter we explain briefly how the economic performance of a CHP plant can be similarly assessed.

5.2 Types of CHP Plant

There are many forms of CHP plant but there are three main types: the pass-out or extraction steam turbine (shown diagrammatically in Figure 5.1), the back-pressure steam turbine (Figure 5.2), and the gas turbine (or diesel engine) feeding a waste heat boiler (WHB) or recuperator (Figure 5.3). A less-popular variation is a complex combined gas turbine/steam turbine plant in which the steam component can be either a back-pressure turbine (Figure

67

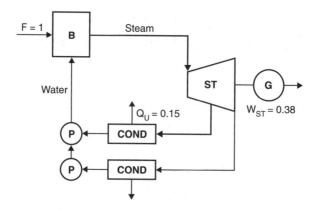

Fig. 5.1. Pass-Out Turbine

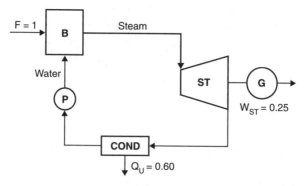

Fig. 5.2. Back-Pressure Turbine

5.4) or a pass-out extraction turbine (Figure 5.5). In each version, the steam turbine not only meets the heat load but also contributes an electrical output, in addition to that of the gas turbine.

The first type, the pass-out turbine, and the fourth and fifth (variations of the CCGT plant), are usually used for very large schemes in cities; the second, the back-pressure steam turbine, is often used for industrial process schemes (such as papermaking); the third, the gas turbine or diesel engine with a WHB, is most popular for small-scale applications (industrial, commercial, and domestic housing).

The figures also show how unit energy supply may be used to meet the demands for heat (Q_D) and work (W_D) in each case. The pass-out turbine (Figure 5.1) may produce some 38% of the primary energy in work but only 15% in useful heat ($\lambda_D = 0.39$). Typically, a back-pressure turbine (Figure 5.2) may produce 25% of the primary energy in work and some 60% in

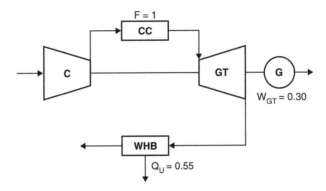

Fig. 5.3. Gas Turbine Plus WHR

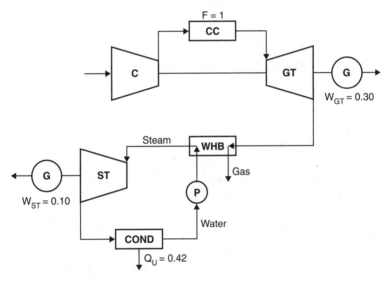

Fig. 5.4. Combined Cycle Gas Turbine CHP Plant a

useful heat, so that $\lambda_D = 2.4$. The gas turbine with a WHB may produce 30% work and 55% useful heat, with $\lambda_D = 1.83$. The first CCGT/back-pressure steam turbine plant illustrated may produce 40% work and 42% heat so that $\lambda_D = 1.05$; the second CCGT/pass-out steam turbine plant may produce less work (0.38%) and less heat (20%) so that $\lambda_D = 0.52$.

These are approximate figures and the performance of particular plants will vary from these representative figures. We discuss their performance in more detail after defining some performance parameters for CHP plants in general.

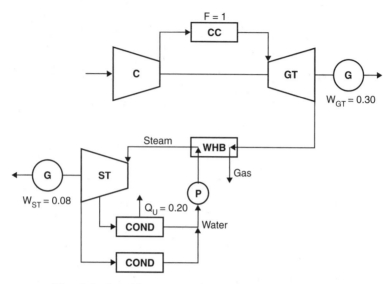

Fig. 5.5. Combined Cycle Gas Turbine CHP Plant b

5.3 Performance Parameters for a CHP Plant

In a CHP plant, heat is rejected at a slightly higher temperature than in the conventional plant so it can be used usefully. This leads to a plant with a smaller thermal efficiency (less work is being delivered because of the higher rejection temperature), but because both useful work and useful work are produced, a higher fraction of the bound energy in the fuel is used. However, as explained in Chapter 2, it is wrong to say that such a CHP plant has a higher thermal efficiency. It does indeed have a higher energy utilisation, since more of the fuel energy is used, but it has a lower thermal efficiency. The energy utilisation factor was defined earlier as

$$(EUF) = (\dot{W} + \dot{Q}_U)/\dot{F} \qquad [5.1]$$

where $\dot{F} = \dot{f}(CV)$ is the rate of supply of energy from a fuel supplied at a rate $\dot{f}$, with calorific value (CV).

Work is more difficult to produce than heat and therefore more highly priced. So a value-weighted energy utilisation factor is sometimes used to take account of the different pricing of electricity and heat. If the sale price of electricity is Y_E and that of heat is Y_H, and the cost of fuel is Z, then this value-weighted energy utilisation factor is

$$(EUF)_{VW} = \frac{Y_E \dot{W} + Y_H \dot{Q}_U}{Z \dot{F}}.$$ [5.2]

Another performance parameter occasionally used is the artificial thermal efficiency in which the energy in the fuel supply to the CHP plant (F) is supposed to be reduced by that which would be required to produce the useful heat ($\dot{Q}_U$) in a separate heat only boiler of efficiency η_B, that is, by ($\dot{Q}_U/\eta_B$). Then the artificial thermal efficiency is

$$\eta_A = W/[\dot{F} - (\dot{Q}_U/\eta_A)] = \eta_{CG}/[1 - (\dot{Q}_U/\eta_B \dot{F})]$$ [5.3]

where $\eta_{CG} = \dot{W}/\dot{F}$.

We use the artificial efficiency in the later discussion of the economics of CHP plants.

5.4 The Pass-out or Extraction Steam Turbine

The pass-out or extraction steam turbine CHP (Fig. 5.1) plant involves a major modification of a Rankine cycle. The basic plant operates at more or less the normal temperatures and pressures, chosen for a power plant of high-thermal efficiency, exhausting to a condenser at low pressure an approximately atmospheric temperature. However, along the casing of the steam turbine, some steam is tapped off at an intermediate pressure, and hence at a temperature at which it can condense, well above atmospheric. The cooling water from this auxiliary condenser can therefore be used in central heating systems in big blocks of housing and, in particular, apartment buildings. There is a degree of flexibility built into this type of plant in that the amount of steam tapped off along the turbine is variable to some extent. This decreases the work output from the plant but it increases the useful heat that is available in the auxiliary condenser.

A large CHP plant of this type, with a considerable degree of sophistication and flexibility, was built in the old USSR in the seventies. Its maximum electrical work output was 250 MW and its corresponding useful heat output was 385 MW, which involved a substantial quantity of extracted steam. It thus had a useful heat-to-work ratio of 1.54, which compares with a much smaller figure, $\lambda_D = 0.39$, in the illustrative sketch of Figure 5.1, where a very much smaller and more usual degree of extraction steam was assumed.

5.5 The Back-Pressure Steam Turbine

Essentially the back-pressure steam turbine (see Fig. 5.2) is based on the normal Rankine steam cycle but with the exhaust at a higher pressure than is adopted for high-efficiency steam power plants. This raises the temperature of the condensing steam to a level where the condenser cooling water can be used, for example, in a hot water space-heating application.

A big back-pressure steam plant was engineered by Sulzer for the Aubrugg heat and power station north of Zurich in Switzerland in 1980. It has three back-pressure turbines each of 45 MW electricity and two additional (heat only) boilers (total 117 MW heat) to meet the extra winter-heat demand. It can supply a total heat load of 465 MW to four districts in the Zurich area. Thus, the heat- to-power ratio of the basic CHP plant is (465 − 117)/(135) = 2.6, as compared to $\lambda_D = 2.4$ as shown in the illustrative sketch of Figure 5.2.

5.6 The Gas Turbine with a Waste Heat Boiler

A gas turbine usually exhausts to atmospheric pressure at relatively high exhaust temperature. This means that here is a heating capacity in the exhaust gases which may be exploited by passing them through a WHB, sometimes called a heat recovery steam generator (HRSG) (Fig. 5.3) to raise steam, usually for industrial processes such as papermaking. Flexibility can be added to this type of plant by supplying additional fuel (usually natural gas), which can be burnt with the excess oxygen in the exhaust gases. This enables the quantity of steam raised to be increased considerably, together with the useful heat delivered.

A small CHP plant of this type was installed at Beilen in the Netherlands using a Ruston gas turbine. The plant produces dairy products, and it replaced a system in which electric power was taken from the national grid and the original heat demand was met by two separate gas-fired boilers. The Ruston gas turbine (rated at 3.65 MW) is able to meet the demand of 3.2 MW. The plant can operate with an unfired HRSG, to supply a heat demand of some 7.5 MW, so that the ratio of useful heat supplied to electrical power is 7.5/3.2 = 2.34, compared with $\lambda_D = 1.83$ shown in the block diagram of Figure 5.3. This ratio can be increased considerably by firing the HRSG so that a heat load of 23 MW can be met with little change in the electric power delivered. The ratio of useful heat to work is then $\lambda_D = 23/3.2 = 7.29$, so that this plant is very flexible. This type of CHP plant can also be operated with a diesel engine or a gas engine as the power plant.

5.7 The CCGT/Back-Pressure Plant

In this CCGT plant, the steam turbine is a back-pressure plant. In the CHP version shown diagrammatically in Figure 5.4, the back-pressure turbine, with raised condenser pressure, may meet quite a high useful heat load indicated in the diagram as 0.42, where it more than matched the total power output of 0.4, from the gas turbine (0.3) plus the steam turbine (0.1), giving $\lambda_D = 1.05$.

5.8 The CCGT/Pass-Out or Extraction Plant

Here a pass-out (extraction) turbine is used in the bottoming Rankine-type cycle (Fig. 5.5). Such a plant was installed many years ago at Saarbrucken; the heat recovery steam generator (HRSG) or waste heat boiler supplying a steam turbine, which had provision for bled steam used to heat water for district heating. Provision was also made for additional fuel supply to the HRSG, so this became a very large and flexible plant meeting a wide range of operating conditions in summer and winter. In operation without additional fuel to the waste heat boiler and steam extraction for the district heating the heat-to-power ratio can be up to $\lambda_D = 1.3$, much higher than our earlier example.

5.9 Comparison of Energy Utilisation Factors (EUF) and λ_D for Two CHP Plants

Figure 5.6, taken from Horlock (1), after Porter and Mastanaiah (2), shows the energy utilisation factors (EUF) for two CHP plants, a back-pressure steam turbine and a gas turbine, against the heat-to-work ratio. Areas of operation for each are shown. The back-pressure turbine can operate over a wide range of λ_D with little change of EUF; as the back pressure is raised so the work output will decrease and the heat output may increase, with little or no variation in energy utilisation. The gas turbine with EUF varying between 0.45 and 0.8 has a more restricted range of λ_D.

5.10 The Economics of CHP Plants

The thermodynamic advantages of these CHP plants are clear but the economics are not immediately obvious. While there are considerable savings in the primary fuel used, and consequently substantial reductions of carbon dioxide produced, a CHP plant will usually require increased capital expen-

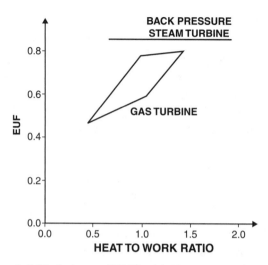

Fig. 5.6. Variations of EUF with Heat-to-Work Ratio

diture to replace existing operational plant. The savings in electricity and fuel costs have to be balanced against the increased cost of the capital required.

It was shown in Chapter 3 (and in more detail in Appendix A) that the annual cost of electricity delivered by a power plant P_E ($ per annum) is given approximately by

$$(P_E = \beta C_0 + M + (OM)) \qquad [5.4]$$

where C_0 is the capital cost of plant (e.g., $); $\beta(i,N)$ is a capital charge factor, which is related to the discount rate (i) on capital and the life of the plant (N years); M is the annual cost of fuel supplied (e.g., $ p.a.); (OM) is the annual cost of operation and maintenance (e.g., $ p.a.).

The "unitised" production cost Y_E ($ per kilowatt hour) for the plant was then written as

$$Y_E = \frac{P_E}{\dot{W}H} = \frac{\beta C_0}{\dot{W}H} + \frac{M}{\dot{W}H} + \frac{(OM)}{\dot{W}H}, \qquad [5.5]$$

which can be developed to give

$$Y_E = \frac{\beta C_0}{\dot{W}H} + \frac{S}{[CV]_0(\eta_0)} + \frac{(OM)}{\dot{W}H} \qquad [5.6]$$

where $\dot{W}$ is the rating of the plant (kW), H is the plant utilisation (hours per annum), S is the unit cost of fuel (\$/kg), $[CV]_0$ is the calorific value (kWh/kg), and $(\eta_O) = \dfrac{\dot{W}}{\dot{F}}$ is the overall efficiency of the plant (η_0), delivering power $\dot{W}$ from fuel energy supplied at a rate $\dot{F}$.

This approach can be developed in several ways to analyse the economics of a CHP plant in comparison with two conventional plants, a power plant and a heat-only boiler, separately supplying similar quantities of useful work and heat. Perhaps the simplest approach is to consider the cogeneration plant (subscript CG) as meeting the electrical demand of the conventional power plant (subscript C) and simply replacing a boiler (subscript B) of capital cost C_B. Then if the unit costs of fuel (S) to the new cogeneration plant and the displaced boiler are the same, the unitised cost of plant CG may be written as

$$Y_E = \frac{\beta C_{CG} - C_B}{\dot{W}H} + \frac{S}{[CV]_0(\eta_A)} + \frac{[(OM)_{CG} - (OM)_B]}{\dot{W}H} \qquad [5.7]$$

where the capital and maintenance cost terms have been reduced by those of the now displaced boiler, and the artificial efficiency η_A defined earlier

$$\eta_A = \dot{W}/[\dot{F} - (\dot{Q}_U/\eta_B)] = \eta_{CG}/[1 - (\dot{Q}_U/\eta_B\dot{F})] \qquad [5.8]$$

This reflects the reduced amount of fuel being used by the CG plant because of the elimination of the separate boiler to provide the useful heat $\dot{Q}_U$. The unitised cost of the electricity $(Y_E)_{CG}$ may then be compared with that for the conventional power plant $(Y_E)_C$ and the savings produced by going to combined heat and power $[(Y_E)_C - (Y_E)_{CG}]$ may be determined. It should be noted that the annual utilisation (H hours) is critical, with the production cost reducing substantially with higher utilisation.

The difficulty of matching CHP plants to both electricity demand and heat demand is illustrated in Table 5.1, taken from Horlock (1) after Kelhofer (3). A comparison is made between four CHP plants—a pass-out turbine (A), a back-pressure turbine (B), a gas turbine with a WHB (C), and a CCGT plant with a back-pressure turbine (D). All four plants are designed to meet a heat demand of 25 kg/s of process steam at 3.5 bar and 190°C. But only the pass-out turbine is able to meet the electricity demand of 45 MW. The others produce less electricity and have to buy in the difference between the demand of 45 MW and their own electricity production.

Table 5.1 Types of CHP Plant

		Pass-out Turbine (A)	Back-Pressure Turbine (B)	Gas Turbine with WHB (C)	CCGT Plant with Back-Pressure Turbine (D)
Net power output	MW	45	15.2	25.8	30.1
EUF		0.43	0.81	0.70	0.75
Additional capital cost over steam boiler	S.fr. (millions)	38.0	10.4	18.0	27.2
Fuel costs	Rp./kWh	6.1	3.23	3.73	3.48
Capital costs	Rp./kWh	1.8	1.46	1.40	1.48
Operating costs	Rp./kWh	0.69	0.21	0.22	0.36
Production cost of electricity	Rp./kWh	8.59	4.90	5.44	5.32
Total cost of electricity	Rp./kWh	8.59	8.15	7.40	5.95

Table 5.1 shows that the EUF of plants B, C, and D is high and illustrates that their electricity production costs are less than that of plant A, which is far higher than that of the other plants. However, when the cost of buying in the make up electricity from the grid for plants B, C, and D is added in, the picture changes. The total electricity cost of the fully matched pass-out turbine is independent of the buy-in cost, which is taken as 10 Rp./kWh, in the example. However, now the total electricity costs of the other plants increase substantially. For the back-pressure plant and the gas turbine with a WHB the cost is not much less than the matched pass-out turbine, but the CCGT plant still has a cost some 20% lower. This example illustrates how difficult it is for a CHP plant to match both heat and electricity demands fully.

Notes on assumptions:
Process heat load (steam) 25 kg/s, 3.5 bar, 190°C
Power demand 45 MW

Utilisation 7,000 hours per year
Discount factor 0.14
Fuel price 7.3 S.fr./GJ. (1 S.fr. = 100 Rp)

It should be emphasised that the approach outlined is much simplified. Differing heat and power loads, diurnal as well summer and winter, would be considered in a full analysis.

5.11 Conclusions

The attractions of cogeneration (CHP) plants are considerable as they save fuel and reduce the production of carbon dioxide. There are several types of plant, the most suitable depending on the application and local circumstances. For example, a CHP plant providing both a large amount of useful heat and a substantial electrical power load to major part of a town or city is usually a steam extraction plant. An industrial plant providing heat for process and a matching electrical load may be a back-pressure steam turbine. A hospital or a university campus may be well served by a gas turbine with a waste heat boiler, but most domestic applications may use a smaller diesel or gas engine fitted with exhaust heat recovery.

The energy utilisation of such CHP plants is high, possibly up to 80%, but the economics is not always so attractive. Much will depend on the variability of the loads (diurnal and seasonal).

References

1. Horlock, J. H., 1997, *Co-generation: Combined heat and power*, Krieger, Melbourne, Fla, 1997.
2. Porter, R. W., and Mastanaiah, K., 1982, Thermal economic analysis of heat-matched industrial cogeneration systems, *Energy*,7(2), 171–187.
3. Kehlhofer, R., 1980, Comparison of power plants for cogeneration of heat and power, *Brown Boveri Review*, 8–80, 504–511.

Chapter 6
Power Plants for Transport

6.1 Introduction

In Chapter 3, a description was given of the major forms of stationary power plants used primarily for the generation of electricity—steam turbine, gas turbine, and nuclear plant. For transport, the power plant itself has to be mobile and fuel also has to be carried with it. While the steam turbine is used for propulsion of large ships, thanks initially to the work of Sir Charles Parsons in the early twentieth century, the gas turbine has also been developed for the latter purpose. Nuclear reactors have been used to provide the propulsive power for submarines and large ships like aircraft carriers, but few have been used for commercial ships. Most trains, although initially powered by reciprocating steam engines, are now driven by diesel/electric engines or are directly electrically powered, drawing the electricity from overhead cables or track lines.

It is the reciprocating internal combustion (IC) engine that provides the power for smaller ships and for land transportation. Burning oil, it operates as a two-stroke diesel power plant with fuel injection and compression-ignition (CI); large diesel engines, supercharged with air to provide extra power, are used in many medium-sized and large ships. Burning petrol (gasoline), and with spark ignition (SI), the internal combustion engine usually operates as a four-stroke power plant, and this form of engine has dominated smaller road transport.

For many years, reciprocating internal combustion (SI) engines also provided power for aircraft, to drive propellers providing forward thrust for the aircraft. Following the Second World War, the gas turbine was adapted to provide the turbojet engine, following the work of Sir Frank Whittle in the United Kingdom and Hans van Ohain in Germany. Basically, instead of using the energy in the exhaust from the gas turbine generator to drive an electric generator, as in the stationary gas turbine power plant, these gases are expanded to high velocity and used to develop forward thrust to propel the aircraft. Since that time, the turbojet engine has come to dominate air transport worldwide.

The major users of primary energy for transport are now the reciprocating internal combustion engine (the SI petrol engine for cars and the CI diesel engine for trucks, lorries, buses, and most ships), and the kerosene-fuelled gas turbine turbojet engine for aircraft. Nearly a fifth of the world's consumption of primary energy is used for transport, but much of this energy is eventually wasted in the engine exhausts.

6.2 The Reciprocating Internal Combustion Engine

Automotives use reciprocating engines and are large consumers of fossil fuels, responsible for a major fraction of the world's consumption of primary energy for transport. As the developing countries expand their economies, the demand for fuel for automotive transport is growing apace, and the pressure on oil resources becomes even heavier. With increasing fuel costs and the requirement of reducing carbon emissions, there is considerable incentive to produce cars with smaller and more efficient engines using less fossil fuel, but there is a growing market for biofuels (see Chapter 8).

In Chapter 2, we briefly described the working stroke of a hypothetical internal combustion engine in our early discussion of how fuel energy can be converted into work. Following combustion at constant volume, the pressure of the gas products dropped, moving a piston in a cylinder, increasing the volume, and doing displacement work. In practice, the combustion process and the working or power stroke can be incorporated into either a four-stroke or a two-stroke engine. The basic operation of a four-stroke engine is illustrated in Figure 6.1.

6.2.1 The Four-Stroke Engine

In the first *intake or suction* stroke, the piston moves down and air and fuel are drawn into the cylinder through inlet valves that have been opened. These valves are then closed and in the second *compression* stroke, the piston moves upward, returning to its original position and compressing the reactants. Combustion takes place at the end of this stroke, the pressure and temperature increasing substantially ready for the third *working or power* stroke, as described in Chapter 2. The exhaust valves then open and the combustion gases are discharged as the piston moves upward again in the *exhaust* stroke.

In the four-stroke *spark ignition* (SI) petrol or gasoline engine, fuel is drawn into the engine with the air in the suction stroke, and combustion is initiated by a spark. In the four-stroke *compression-ignition* (CI) engine it is

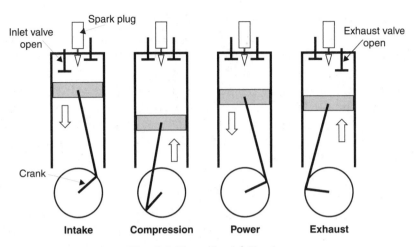

Fig. 6.1. Four-Stroke Engine

air only that is drawn into the engine through the inlet valves in the suction stroke, the fuel (diesel oil) being separately injected at or near the end of the compression stroke by a fuel pump. The compression is greater than in the petrol engine so the air temperature after compression is higher than in the petrol engine; combustion is spontaneous, no spark being required.

6.2.2 The Two-Stroke Engine

In the two-stroke engine, the working stroke and the exhaust stroke of the four-stroke engine are essentially combined, exhaust beginning well before the end of a first working stroke. The suction stroke and the compression stroke are similarly combined into a single return stroke, the inlet valve opening early so that inlet and exhaust valves are open simultaneously for a short overlap period, during which a "scavenge" process cleans out the exhaust replacing it with fresh air, sometimes with the help of a supercharger. Small two-stroke power plants may use petrol or gasoline and require crankcase compression of the air before it enters the cylinder. The two-stroke system is more frequently used in larger diesel engines with fuel injection and requiring supercharging of the air. The supercharger may be driven by the exhaust gases in a multicylinder power plant.

6.2.3 Air Standard Cycles

As emphasised, internal combustion power plants are not heat engines in the strict thermodynamic sense. However, hypothetical heat engines using fixed quantities of air as the working fluid can be used to "match" internal combustion power plants, externally supplied heat and external rejection of heat replacing the combustion process and the exhaust process respectively. These heat engines are said to operate on "air standard cycles" and they are useful in analysing the performance of the practical IC engines, which they simulate, particularly in the deduction of the important parameters that affect that performance. The efficiency of the air standard cycle (η_{CY}) gives some guidance to the overall efficiency of the corresponding practical power plant it simulates.

The real plant overall efficiency is

$$\eta_O = \dot{W}/\dot{f}\,(CV) \qquad\qquad [6.1]$$

where $\dot{W} = BP$ is the brake power (BP) delivered by the engine, $\dot{f}$ is the flow rate of the fuel and (CV) is its calorific value. The "specific fuel consumption" of the engine is usually expressed as the fuel consumption rate $\dot{f}$ divided by the BP and so it is inversely proportional to the overall efficiency of the plant (η_O). However, although the operation of the real power plant can be simulated to some extent by a corresponding air standard cycle, (η_O) is less than (η_{CY}) because of frictional and other losses.

6.2.3.1 The Otto Constant Volume Cycle

Figure 6.2 illustrates on a pressure-volume diagram the Otto constant volume (air standard) cycle undergone by air contained in a cylinder. Starting at state 1, the air is compressed to state 2, where heat is added at constant cylinder volume and the temperature (and pressure) increase to state 3. The air is then expanded to state 4, and heat is then extracted at constant volume to restore the working fluid to state 1. There is no flow in or out and the closed cycle can be repeated.

Thus the combustion and exhaust processes of the practical power plant have been replaced by heating supply and rejection in the air standard cycle. The nett work output is the work delivered in expansion less the work input required for compression; these processes are similar to those in the real engine. But in the air standard cycle they are assumed to be adiabatic with no heat transfers and are perfect "reversible" processes, whereas in the real engine there is heat loss to the cooling water in the jacket round the cylinder and piston friction.

It is a straightforward matter to analyse the air standard Otto cycle, de-

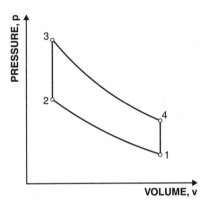

Fig. 6.2. Otto Cycle

termining its classical heat engine efficiency (η_{CY}) as the work output divided by heat supplied. Referring to Figure 6.2, (η_{CY}) may be shown to be a function of a single performance parameter, the volumetric compression ratio ($r_v = v_1/v_2$),

$$(\eta_{CY})_{OTTO} = f(r_v) \qquad [6.2]$$

and this relation is plotted in the upper lines of Figures 6.4a and b. It is seen that efficiency increases with the compression ratio, but in the practical engine the overall efficiency will be less, and material and mechanical considerations will impose limitations.

6.2.3.2 The Diesel Cycle

In the Diesel air standard cycle (Fig. 6.3) the heating process is different from that of the Otto cycle. After compression from state 1 to state 2 the combustion process of the real engine is now simulated in the air standard cycle by a constant pressure heating process (from state 2 to state 3), during which a modest increase in volume (v_2 to v_3) takes place before the main adiabatic expansion continues, to state 4. The exhaust process of the practical engine is then simulated by a constant volume cooling process in the Diesel air standard cycle, as in the Otto cycle.

The efficiency of the Diesel air standard cycle is illustrated in Figures 6.4a and b. The efficiency is a function not only of the volumetric compression ratio r_v but also the so-called cut-off ratio $r_c = v_3/v_2$,

$$(\eta_{CY})_{DIESEL} = f(r_v, r_c) \qquad [6.3]$$

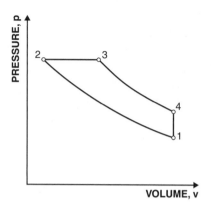

Fig. 6.3. Diesel Cycle

Figures 6.4*a* and *b* show that as the cut-off ratio is decreased so the diesel air standard cycle efficiency approaches that of the Otto air standard efficiency. For a given compression ratio, the Otto cycle efficiency is always greater than that of the Diesel cycle.

6.2.3.3 The Dual Cycle

In a variation of the air standard cycles described above, usually called the dual cycle, the heating process is different from those of the Otto and Diesel cycles. (See Figure 6.5, which shows the pressure volume diagram for the dual air standard cycle.) After compression from state 1 to state 2 the combustion process of the real engine is now simulated by a constant volume heating process (from state 2 to state 3) followed by constant pressure heating process (from state 3 to state 3A) before the main adiabatic expansion continues, to state 4. The exhaust process of the practical engine is then simulated by a constant volume cooling process.

This cycle more closely simulates the combustion process in a real Diesel engine, the first heating process corresponding to fuel injection and partial combustion, at constant volume, and the second constant pressure process simulating the remaining combustion. The air standard dual cycle efficiency is now a function of r_v, r_c, and $r_p = p_3/p_2$,

$$(\eta_{CY})_{CY} = f(r_v, r_c, r_p) \qquad [6.4]$$

and will lie between the Otto and Diesel air standard efficiencies, for the same compression ratio and heat supply.

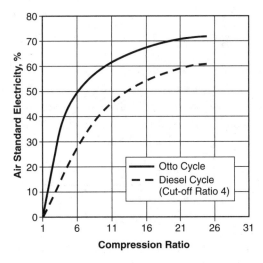

Fig. 6.4. *a*, Otto and Diesel Cycle Efficiency

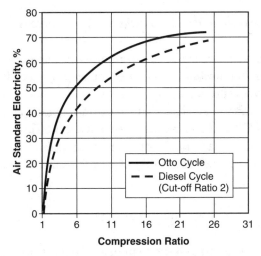

Fig. 6.4. *b*, Otto and Diesel Cycle Efficiency

6.2.4 Performance of IC engines

The internal combustion engine is a remarkably compact and robust power source engine and has had few competitors for automobiles. The fuel consumption of the IC engine varies with its size, and we measure the capacity of the engine by the volume of the cylinders. Thus a single cylinder motor cycle engine may have a capacity of two or three hundred cubic

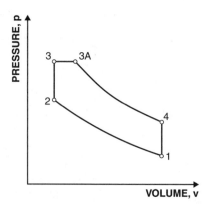

Fig. 6.5. Dual Cycle

centimetres, but a big Jaguar engine with six cylinders will rate as three or four thousand ccs. The amount of fuel used will in general increase with the size of the engine.

6.2.4.1 Comparison of Real IC Engine Performance with Air Standard Cycles

While the air standard cycles give a guide to the theoretical performance of IC engines further discussion of real engine performance is required (see Rogers and Mayhew [1]).

The first major point is that practical engine overall performance is defined in terms of several efficiencies—first, overall efficiency, second, the indicated efficiency, and third, the mechanical efficiency.

The overall thermal efficiency is defined as it has been for heat engines generally

$$\eta_o = \dot{W}/\dot{f}\,(CV) \qquad [6.5]$$

where $\dot{W} = BP$ is the (brake) power output and $\dot{f}$ is the mass flow of fuel of calorific value (CV). Since in engine tests the power is developed through the brake where it can be measured the overall efficiency for an IC engine is often called the brake thermal efficiency $\eta_b.$

This brake efficiency can be the further defined as the product of the indicated efficiency η_I and the mechanical efficiency $\eta_m,$

$$\eta_b = \eta_I\,\eta_m \qquad [6.6]$$

The indicated power could be calculated from the real pressure volume (p,v)

indicator diagram of the engine, which is comparable to that of the corresponding air standard cycle; although there are important differences (see later below). If the real *pv* diagram is known then integration round the cycle gives an indicated mean effective pressure p_I and this then gives the indicated power.

$$IP = p_I LAN \qquad [6.7]$$

where A is piston area, L is engine stroke, and N is the number of machine cycles per unit time—half the rotational speed for a four-stroke engine and the rotational speed for a two-stroke engine.

But the indicated power has to overcome mechanical losses before the power reaches the brake, and these losses are reflected in the mechanical efficiency η_m, which might be of the order of 85–90% for an engine on full load. Thus, the brake power is

$$BP = \eta_m IP \qquad [6.8]$$

and the corresponding brake mean effective pressure p_b is given by

$$BP = p_b LAN \qquad [6.9]$$

with

$$p_b = \eta_m p_I \qquad [6.10]$$

There are several reasons for the differences between the processes in the real engine and the theoretical air standard cycle (see [1]. They include

a. The real processes are not so clearly delineated in the real indicator diagram as in the air standard cycle. For example the time taken for valves to open are finite so the corners on the real diagrams are rounded off.

b. Temperature changes levels are quite large (the maximum transient gas temperature may be as high as 2,800 K in an IC engine). So variations in specific heats come into play compared with ideal air processes and dissociation effects are present.

c. The use of cylinder cooling means that the compression and expansion processes are not adiabatic.

d. For the four-stroke engine, the air standard cycles are modified to show two almost horizontal lines near atmospheric pressure representing the suction and exhaust strokes of the real engine. They enclose a small area that represents the pumping power lost in these strokes.

6.3 The Turbojet Engine

How much fuel an aircraft needs for a flight depends on its drag (which must be overcome by the engine thrust, T) and its flight path, altitude, and range (see Cumpsty [2]). The performance of the propelling engine system is usually assessed in terms of two parameters, the thrust force it develops and its specific fuel consumption, usually expressed as the fuel flow rate ($\dot{f}$) (divided by the engine thrust (T), $sfc = \dot{f}/T$.

An alternative to the specific fuel consumption is the "overall" flight efficiency (η_O), which is the power supplied to the aircraft (the product of the thrust force T and the flight velocity, [V]) divided by the fuel energy supplied to the engine, $\dot{f}(CV)$, where (CV) is the calorific value of the fuel. Thus,

$$\eta_O = TV/\dot{f}(CV) = V/[sfc(CV)] \qquad [6.11]$$

But this overall flight performance essentially involves two performance parameters, the propulsive efficiency (η_P) and the "thermal" efficiency (η_{TH}) of the simple turbojet engine (Figure 6.6), which is based on the internal combustion gas turbine power plant (described in section 3.3.1). After the products of combustion expand through the turbine, driving the compressor, there is surplus energy available in the turbojet application; instead of driving a generator as in the stationary power plant, these gases are accelerated to high jet velocity (V_j, relative to the engine) in a final nozzle and used to propel an aircraft at the flight velocity V.

From Newton's law of momentum, the thrust produced by the engine is the change in momentum of the fluid passing through the engine. In a turbojet engine the fuel flow is small compared to the air flow so that the thrust is approximately ($V_j - V$) per unit air flow. The propulsive efficiency is now introduced; it is defined as the ratio of the power delivered to the aircraft— the product of the thrust and the flight velocity, ($V_j - V$)V, to the increase in kinetic energy across the engine ($V_j^2 - V^2$)/2, both per unit air flow. Thus the propulsive efficiency is given by

$$\eta_P = \frac{(V_j - V)V}{(V_j^2 - V^2)/2} = \frac{2V}{(V_j + V)} = \frac{2}{[1 + (V_j/V)]} \qquad [6.12]$$

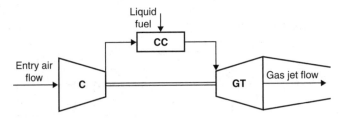

Fig. 6.6. Turbojet Engine

This expression shows that the smaller the increase in velocity across the engine $(V_j - V)$ the higher the propulsive efficiency; however, this is achieved at the expense of lower thrust per unit flow rate. (Murphy's law to an engineer!)

But the "thermal" efficiency of the engine (η_{TH}) is defined as the ratio of the increase in kinetic energy across the engine divided by the fuel energy supplied,

$$\eta_{TH} \approx \frac{V_j^2 - V^2}{2 \dot{f}(CV)} \tag{6.13}$$

Hence, the overall flight efficiency is the product of the propulsive efficiency and the thermal efficiency

$$\eta_O = \eta_P \eta_{TH} = \{\frac{(V_j - V)}{\dot{f}(CV)}\} = \frac{V}{sfc(CV)} \tag{6.14}$$

The designer of an aircraft jet engine wishes to achieve both high thermodynamic performance in his basic gas turbine (high η_{TH} and low fuel consumption) and high η_P (relatively low jet velocity in comparison with the flight velocity). This is achieved in the modern bypass engine (Figure 6.7) in which air is bypassed round the engine to meet the turbine exhaust gases in a final nozzle, lowering the value of the mean final jet velocity V_j. This type of engine not only has higher propulsive efficiency but it also has lower jet noise; it has swept the field in commercial transport aircraft in the past thirty years.

The reader is referred to the excellent and readable book by Cumpsty (2) for more detailed information on turbojet engines.

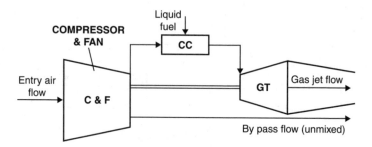

Figure 6.7 Bypass Engine

References

1. Rogers, G.F.C. and Mayhew, Y. Engineering Thermodynamics, Longman, 4th edition, 1992.
2. Cumpsty, N.A. Jet Propulsion, Krieger, Melbourne, Fla. 2006.

Chapter 7
Pollution and Global Warming

7.1 Introduction

Until recent years, the main concerns relating to primary energy have been the rate at which it is used, the finite nature of the fossil fuel resources, and the time that such resources would remain available. Thus, the major criterion for the performance of power plants was attainment of high thermal efficiency to reduce use of primary energy—coupled with its effect on reducing costs, both of electricity production for stationary power plants and transport for mobile power plants. In the use of fossil fuels for heating devices, high "boiler" efficiencies were similarly important in restricting the consumption of primary energy.

Now a further criterion of performance has been introduced: the amount of carbon dioxide produced by power plants and heating devices, as this gas makes a major contribution to global warming. Critical in the production of CO_2 is the type of fuel used in the plant. For a nuclear power plant there is virtually no carbon dioxide production, and for some renewables, such as wind, hydro and tidal power, there is none at all, except in the course of construction. It is the fossil fuels that are the guilty parties.

Carbon dioxide (CO_2) is produced when the carbon content of a fuel joins with oxygen in the air supply, and the CO_2 is later discharged to the atmosphere. Thus coal, with a high carbon content, is the biggest producer of CO_2 per unit of chemical energy liberated in combustion. Natural gas consists mainly of methane, which is 75% carbon by mass and 25% hydrogen. In combustion, the carbon and the hydrogen combine with oxygen in the air and both these reactions contribute to the liberation of chemical energy, raising the temperature of the products of combustion. For natural gas, the amount of carbon dioxide formed per unit of chemical energy liberated (usually taken as the calorific value) is less than that in the combustion of coal, so that it is a cleaner fuel than coal in this respect. Fuel oils fall in between the two in this new measure of performance, as is illustrated in Figure 7.1.

Another pollutant is sulphur dioxide, which is formed when the sulphur

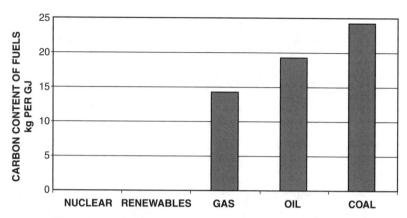

Fig. 7.1. Carbon Dioxide Produced from Combustion
of Fossil Fuels per Unit of Heat Liberated

content of a fuel, particularly that present in some types of coal, is combined with oxygen in combustion and discharged to the atmosphere. This leads to acid rain falling from clouds and to destruction of plant life and vegetation. Measures have been taken in Europe and elsewhere to reduce this form of pollution; it is carbon dioxide that is the main focus of attention currently, and which is our concern here. However, as India and China have expanded their economies, using large amounts of "dirty" coal, so sulphur dioxide and acid rain have become more important again, mainly in Asia.

7.2 The Greenhouse Effect and the Carbon Cycle

The level of concentration of carbon dioxide in the atmosphere influences the reflection back of radiation from the earth and this affects the earth's temperature. Incoming short wave length solar radiation passes easily through the atmosphere but much of the outgoing longer wave length thermal radiation is absorbed by CO_2 (and water vapour), acting like a blanket. It is analogous to the effect found in greenhouses where the glass and moist air lets in the sunlight but prevents heat escaping, hence the use of the term greenhouse gases in describing the effect of CO_2 in the atmosphere.

The supply of man-made carbon dioxide from the burning of fossil fuels (E) has to be seen in relation to the overall carbon cycle, which is complex. This is illustrated in Figure 7.2 as originally illustrated many years ago for an Open University course by Brown and Skipsey (1) and used implicitly by many others since then (e.g., Socolow and Lam and the Princeton research group [2]). Besides the atmosphere (C), there are three other car-

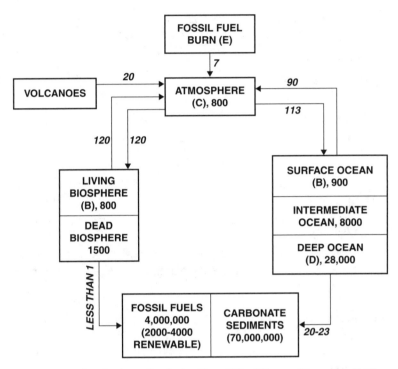

Fig. 7.2. The Carbon Cycle in Simplified Form, Showing GtC

bon "reservoirs": the biosphere/shallow oceans (B), the deep oceans (D), and carbonate sediments and fossil fuels below the ground. There is a natural, almost balanced, circulation between these as is shown in the diagram; the flows of carbon per annum between the reservoirs are the figures shown in italic. Photosynthesis and biochemical delay circulate CO_2 in the birth-life-death cycles of the biosphere and the dissolution of CO_2 in surface waters and ground waters leads to precipitation of carbonate rich sediments.

Disturbance of this naturally balanced carbon cycle follows from the introduction of volcanic gases from the earth's interior and combustion of fossil fuels. The atmospheric reservoir contains about 800 gigatonnes of carbon, or 800 GtC; volcanic gases supply about 20 GtC of carbon per year, and man-made fossil fuel combustion (E) adds about a third of the volcanic contribution (7 GtC). This is a much simplified picture and the changes in carbon dioxide taking place are extremely complex and generally difficult to calculate; the effects of water vapour and cloud formation must also be taken into account although they are uncertain.

It is clear that the molar concentration (or parts per million by volume, ppmv) of carbon dioxide in the atmosphere, which was about 280 ppmv in

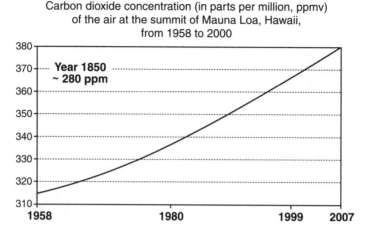

Fig. 7.3. Carbon Dioxide Concentration in the Atmosphere over the Latter Half of the Twentieth Century at the Summit of Mauna Loa, Hawaii

the mid-nineteenth century, has risen to a current value of nearly 380 ppmv. Figure 7.3 shows the carbon dioxide concentrations measured at the summit of Mauna Los in Hawaii over the period 1958–1999, with the addition of a figure for 1850.

The relationship between atmospheric concentrations of CO_2 in ppmv and the carbon content C is

$$1 \text{ ppmv} \cong 2.1 \text{ GtC.}$$

Socolow and Lam (2) refer to this relation as the Rosetta stone of climate change. These authors presented a useful straightforward analysis of the carbon cycle some of which we reproduce in Appendix B. There, instead of assuming that the rate of increase in $C(t)$ is simply proportional to fossil fuel emissions $E(t)$,

$$dC/dt = kE, \tag{7.1}$$

with k is of the order of one half, they allow for three tanks (C, B, and D) with leakage flows between them, and are able to derive simple expressions for the rate of change of atmospheric concentrations in comparison with elaborate computer solutions. We shall discuss the results of Socolow and Lam later, together with their recommendations for future energy policy.

At this stage, we present a simplified picture of the magnitude of the problem as portrayed by the Princeton group (Figures 7.4a and b). Fig-

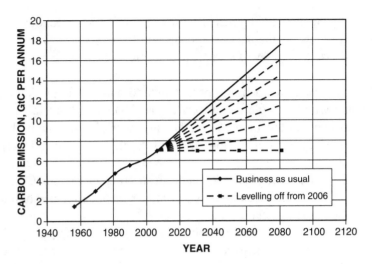

Fig.7.4. *a*, Annual Carbon Emissions and Potential Levelling-off

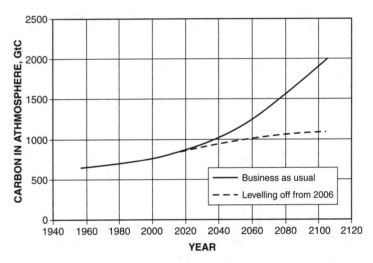

Fig. 7.4. *b*, Cumulative Atmospheric Carbon

ure 7.4*a* shows that if carbon emissions from fossil fuels continue to grow as they have done over the past fifty years they will reach about 14 GtC per annum in 2056. This will then produce some 1,200 GtC of carbon in the atmosphere, as shown in Figure 7.4*b*. This corresponds to a concentration of about 570 ppmv of carbon dioxide, approximately doubling the preindustrial level.

The global temperature rise that would result remains a matter of much scientific discussion. But the United Nations Intergovernmental Panel on Climate Change (IPCC) recently estimated that the greenhouse effect could be to increase the average global temperatures by between 2° and 4.5°C and that at such levels severe adverse climatic change consequences are likely.

International agreement has been sought to limit future production of carbon and with it the global temperature rise. There are several ways in which this can be done (some of which have been given publicity by the film produced by Senator Al Gore, former U.S. presidential candidate):

a. By demand modification, that is, restricting our demands for heat, electricity and transport (e.g., by improving insulation in buildings and reducing heat losses, by travelling less, etc.);

b. By supply modification, that is, by improving the efficiency of fossil fuel energy conversion (increasing the thermal efficiency of power plants and the boiler efficiency of heating devices);

c. By replacing fossil fuel heat and power plants with renewable plants (wind, hydro, tidal power production, and solar heating);

d. By modification of the so-called carbon cycle, introducing fast-growing energy crops, which rapidly absorb carbon dioxide from the atmosphere, to replace the use of the fossil fuels, coal, oil, and natural gas;

e. By replacing these high-carbon fossil fuels with lower or even a zero-carbon fuel (hydrogen);

f. Separating carbon dioxide from the exhaust products of fossil fuel plants, pressurising and liquefying it, and storing it deep in the earth or the oceans (a process known as carbon sequestration and storage [CSS]).

Reducing the consumption of primary fuel energy and the production of carbon dioxide, mainly by the actions a. and b., is loosely referred to as increasing the energy efficiency overall. (We shall discuss how energy efficiency can be increased in Chapter 9, but first we consider here the coupling between energy consumption and carbon dioxide production.) It has to be said that the task before us all is enormous and is being underestimated by many people throughout the world.

7.3 Carbon Dioxide Production and the Kyoto Protocol

The world's consumption of fossil fuels was detailed in Chapter 1 and the way that the concentration of carbon dioxide in the earth's atmosphere (in

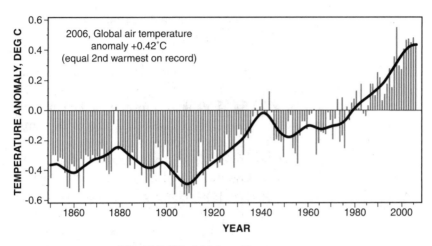

Fig. 7.5. World Mean Temperature

parts per million) has changed is illustrated in Figures 7.4a and b. The marked increase in carbon dioxide concentration since 1950 is clearly paralleled by the increase in fossil fuel consumption over that period. Changes in world mean temperatures are also shown in Figure 7.5 (relative to 1979: data produced by the University of East Anglia and the United Kingdom Hadley Center).

The world's climatologists are deeply involved in predicting the future relationship between CO_2 concentration and global temperatures by studying the past records and extrapolating them into the future. This involves complex analysis and computation, but the scientific community now generally agrees that there is a link between fossil fuel use and global warming and that carbon dioxide production from fossil fuels must be restricted. The Intergovernmental Panel on Climate Change (IPCC) concluded in 2007 that

"most of the observed increase in globally averaged temperatures since the mid-twentieth century is very likely due to the observed increase in anthropogenic greenhouse gas concentrations, which leads to warming of the surface and lower atmosphere by increasing the greenhouse effect."

At the Kyoto conference in 1990, a group of nations agreed to limit their production of carbon within greenhouse gases. The objective of the so-called Kyoto protocol was to reduce the production of a "basket" of greenhouse gases, which lead to global warming (mainly carbon dioxide, so an equivalent CO_2 concentration is used for convenience) and to set targets for such reductions. A summary of the agreement is

"The Kyoto Protocol is an agreement under which industrialised countries will reduce their collective emissions of greenhouse gases by 5.2% compared to the year 1990 (but note that, compared to the emissions levels that would be expected by 2010 without the Protocol, this target represents a 29% cut). The goal is to lower overall emissions of six greenhouse gases—carbon dioxide, methane, nitrous oxide, sulfur hexafluoride, HFCs, and PFCs—calculated as an average over the five-year period of 2008–12. National targets range from 8% reductions for the European Union and some others to 7% for the US, 6% for Japan, 0% for Russia, and permitted increases of 8% for Australia and 10% for Iceland."

Within the European Union, targets were allocated to member states. For example, the United Kingdom was initially committed to decreasing its 1990 production of 210 million tonnes of carbon to about 184 million tonnes in 2010, a reduction of 12.5%. Subsequently, the U.K. government declared an improved objective of a 20% reduction by 2010, but now it appears probable that such a target will be accepted by the whole European Union (EU). Further negotiations are being held to obtain worldwide agreement on future targets.

7.4 Actions in the United Kingsom Following Kyoto

This section illustrates how one European country (the United Kingdom) has set about achieving substantial reductions in CO_2 production since Kyoto.

A major contribution was made by the switching the production of coal-fired power stations to new gas-fired combined cycle plants (although this was already in hand because of the reduced generation costs of these plants and the increased allowability of use of natural gas for power production). Not only are CCGT plants of higher efficiency as was shown in Chapter 3, but the natural gas fuel (mainly methane) produces much less CO_2 per unit of chemical energy liberated than coal (some 60%), as illustrated in Figure 7.1.

Other steps have been taken in the United Kingdom towards the Kyoto target. Some progress has been made in the installation of relatively small-scale combined heat and power (CHP). Another contribution has been the introduction of more renewable generation particularly from wind turbines.

The latter was assisted by the introduction of a government regulation, initially called the nonfossil fuel obligation (NFFO), that required generating companies to provide some 10% of generation from renewable sources. Such generation is more expensive than gas-fired generation (primarily because of the large plant costs in £/kW; see the discussion on generation costs in Chapter 3 and Appendix A), and as a result of the NFFO, the average price of electricity generated in the United Kingdom has gone up. Thus, the cost of this action in reducing carbon dioxide has been borne by the consumer in the United Kingdom.

The United Kingdom has also introduced other fiscal methods including carbon trading, which is referred to in section 7.6. Increased taxation on transport vehicles (both of liquid fuels and of engines with larger capacity and higher fuel consumption) has not yet been markedly successful. Reduction of the carbon production from transport in the United Kingdom has not been substantial, if at all, as the number of vehicles has increased. It appears that this market is inelastic and consumption is not reduced by increased pricing.

Progress has also been made with reduction of energy consumption in industry and in domestic buildings (by better insulation), but the main contribution has been the switch from coal to gas firing of generating plants.

7.5 Other Countries

The pattern of carbon reduction around the world varies greatly from one country to another. Broadly, the European countries mirror the progress made in the United Kingdom, those from the old eastern block making significant reductions, but the biggest producer of carbon dioxide, the United States, has not acted at a national level. The United States did not subscribe to Kyoto and has adhered to a policy of solving the problem in the longer term by new developments on technology. However, individual states, such as California, are taking more immediate action to reduce carbon pollution.

Perhaps the most worrying prospects have been those associated with the two largest countries in the world, China and India, which are increasing the output of carbon dioxide as their economies expand rapidly. For example, China is building many new coal-fired power stations and this is a major reason for the very large increase in coal consumption in China. Figure 7.6a shows the change in Chinese coal production the past twenty years, an increase of some 76% since 1998 and of 11% from 2004 to 2005 alone. Figure 7.6b shows Chinese electricity generation in GW since 1948 with a projection for 2020. Not all of the new generating capacity will be coal-fired as China has plans for large CCGT plants; it is also planning a substantial IGCC (with CCS) programme.

In 2005, the United States and China produced 22% and 18%, respectively, of the world's manmade carbon, but it will not be long before China overtakes the States.

7.6 Fiscal Methods—Carbon Taxing and Carbon Trading

There has been much discussion in Europe about fiscal means of reducing carbon production. The most obvious action would be to introduce a carbon tax, which will effectively add to the price of fuel (resulting in a bigger increase for coal than for natural gas). The economics of electric power generation would then be affected considerably by the amount of CO_2 produced and the level of any environmental penalty imposed by a carbon or carbon dioxide tax.

Thus, for electrical power stations, a new measure of the performance is the amount of CO_2 produced per unit of electricity generated, that is, $\lambda = $ kg(CO_2)/kWh. This quantity can be nondimensionalised by writing $\lambda' = \lambda(16)/44)(LCV)$, where $(16/44)$ is the mass ratio of fuel to CO_2 for methane, the main constituent of natural gas, and (LCV) is its lower heating value. However, presenting the plant's "green" performance directly, in terms of λ, rather than λ', allows the cost of any tax on the carbon dioxide to be added directly to the untaxed cost of electricity production, say in cents per kilowatt hour (c/kWh).

Figure 7.7 shows values of CO_2 emissions in (kg/kWh) plotted against thermal efficiency for a high-carbon fuel plant (conventional coal-fired or IGCC) and a lower-carbon fuel station (natural gas). It illustrates the two obvious routes towards the desired low production of greenhouse gases: seeking high thermal efficiency and using lower carbon fuel.

Although the economics of any particular electric power plant are not yet affected directly by the amount of CO_2 produced, a degree of environmental penalty is likely to be involved in the future, possibly by a carbon or carbon dioxide tax. For example, suppose a CCGT plant of 54% thermal efficiency delivers electricity at an untaxed generating cost of 3.6 c/kWh and produces CO_2 at a rate of 0.3 kg/kWh, as indicated in Figure 7.7. If a carbon dioxide tax were set at $50/tonne of CO_2 (5 c/kg CO_2), then effectively 1.5 p/kWh would be added to the cost of generation, making it 5.1 kWh. This may make the plant uneconomic in comparison with a nuclear station, or even windmills. This point is illustrated in Figure 7.8, which shows how the generation cost for this CCGT plant in c/kWh would vary

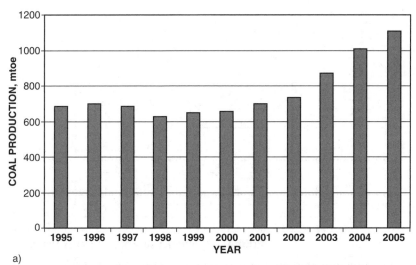

a)

Fig. 7.6. *a*, Coal Comsumption in China Over Recent Years

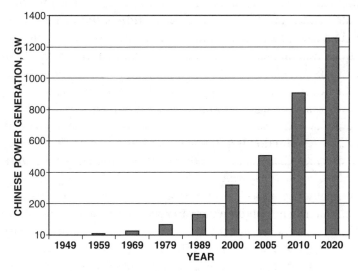

b)

Fig. 7.6. *b*, Chinese Power Generation, GW

with the tax level and how other types of plant might then come into competition with it.

However, suppose that the original CCGT plant were modified to reduce the amount of CO_2 entering the atmosphere from the plant (say to 0.15 kg/kWh) at an additional capital cost, which led to an increase in the untaxed cost of electricity (say from 3.6 to 4.2 c/kWh). Then the effect of a

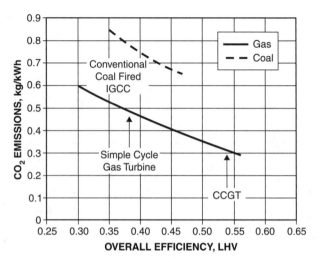

Fig. 7.7. Carbon Dioxide Emissions Per kWh

carbon dioxide tax of 5c/kWh would be to increase the electricity price to $(4.2 + 0.15.5) = 4.95$ c/kWh and this is below the taxed cost of the original plant of 5.1 c/kWh. In fact, the new plant would become economic at a carbon dioxide tax of T c/kg CO_2, given by

$$(3.6 + 0.3T) = (4.2 + 0.15T),$$

that is, when $T = 4$c/kg CO_2.

However, it appears unlikely that such carbon taxes will be introduced widely. More favoured is an alternative fiscal measure, carbon trading, and such a measure has already been introduced in Europe. The basis of the scheme is that participants are given initial certificates for a certain amount of carbon production. If they produce more carbon, then they have to buy additional certificates from other participants who are producing less than their certificated quantities; if they produce less, then they can sell their certificates to other participants who are producing more.

Such schemes can operate on a national basis, the participants being individual countries trading with each other, or they can operate within a country, the participants being different industries. There is currently much discussion about whether airlines should be included in a carbon trading scheme but this is fraught with difficulty in that airlines operate between countries, taking on fuel and taking off in one country and flying over and landing in others.

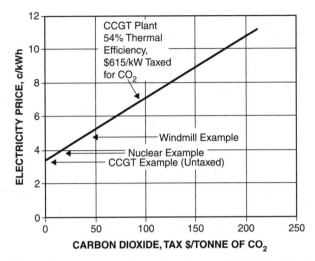

Fig. 7.8. Variation of Generation Cost with Carbon Tax

Carbon trading schemes form an alternative to the introduction of direct carbon taxes, and at present appear to be more favoured by industry and governments. But they are unlikely to be successful on a major scale unless governments impose progressively strict reductions in the CO_2 production allowable in certification, and the jury is out on this.

Another fiscal method gaining recognition and popularity is carbon off-setting, by companies or by individuals. In this scheme, the carbon dioxide produced by a particular action (e.g., taking a long haul flight) is offset by purchasing or contributing to other actions to reduce carbon dioxide production (e.g., buying and planting fast-growing trees or crops to absorb an corresponding amount of the greeenhouse gas, or contributing to new technological research programmes aimed at reduction of carbon dioxide production). While satisfying for the conscience of an individual and/or providing good publicity for a company or industry, the impact is likely to be uncertain. The carbon production is direct and immediate but the remedial action is less measurable in its effect and only takes place after a period of some years.

7.7 Carbon Sequestration and Storage (CSS)

Another technique for dealing with the carbon dioxide problem is carbon sequestration and storage (CSS), but it has not yet been implemented on a large scale.

Carbon dioxide can be captured before or after combustion. In a conventional power station, coal or gas-fired, carbon dioxide can be removed from the exhaust gases by absorbing CO_2 chemically and then regenerating it, so that it can be compressed and suitably stored. The disadvantage of this capture is that carbon dioxide is diluted in the flue gas by nitrogen, water vapour, and other chemicals, which makes consequent extraction difficult.

A second technique involves precombustion separation. In a plant using natural gas, the fuel is first partially oxidised, producing hydrogen and carbon monoxide. A further shift reaction then converts the carbon monoxide to dioxide with the production of more hydrogen. The carbon dioxide is then removed (using physical or chemical absorption), and stored before combustion. The hydrogen-rich fuel gas is burned in a combined cycle gas turbine (CCGT) system capable of accommodating high-burning velocity hydrogen. Alternatively, it could be used in a fuel cell system. These combinations of technologies promise conversion efficiencies approaching 60% without capture, and 48% with capture.

An extension of the precombustion technique for sequestration can be applied to a particular type of coal-fired plant, the integrated gasification combined cycle (IGCC) plant. In this plant, coal, with water addition, is gasified in a separate process and the resultant gas fed into the combustion chamber of the gas turbine in a combined cycle plant. Fitting such IGCC plants with special physical absorption technology to capture carbon dioxide at the precombustion stage is probably the most promising and sustainable technology, as described earlier in Chapter 3. Once the CO_2 has been captured and compressed to liquid form it can be stored in various ways, for example, in deep saline aquifers and depleted oil and gas reservoirs. Several small storage schemes are already in operation.

It is estimated that there are hundreds of years worth of storage capacity in deep saline aquifers, some with capacities of 10,000 Gt of carbon dioxide available; around 920 could be stored in depleted oil and gas fields. However, public acceptance for underground storage in inhabited areas may prove difficult to obtain because of potential leakage.

In addition to undermining the purpose of a storage project, CO_2 leakage from an underground reservoir into the atmosphere could have local effects: ground and water displacement, groundwater contamination, and biological interactions.

7.8 The Longer Term

There has been a growing appreciation of the severity of the global warming problem in recent years and this has resulted in much more ambitious objectives being set for the reduction in man-made carbon and carbon dioxide pollution.

For example, one such ambitious target has been detailed by the United Kingdom Royal Commission on Environmental Pollution (3) to reduce carbon dioxide production from the 1990 levels by 60% by the year 2050, and it has gained some endorsement as a longer term aim more widely around the world. This imposes an incredibly difficult task and would involve major changes in lifestyle.

The major point must be made again: that at the present rate of growth, emissions of carbon dioxide will double by about 2056, as was indicated in Figure 7.3, and the atmospheric concentration of the gas at about 560 ppmv will be about double the preindustrial level. In Chapter 9, we discuss several future energy scenarios, in particular, the arguments of the Princeton group (2) that the world must begin to flatten out these emissions *now*. If it then continues to "ramp" them down (which will involve many substantial actions), it should be possible to keep the critical concentration below the critical 560 ppmv figure. Such proposed actions (which we list in Chapter 9) are drastic indeed but they would still mean that the world temperature in 2056 could on average be 2°C higher than it is now and the climatic changes could be large.

References

1. Brown, G. C., and Skipsey, E., 1986, *Energy resources*, Open University Press, Milton Keynes.
2. Socolow, R. H., and Lam, H., 2007, Good enough tools for global warming policy making, Phil. Trans Royal Society A, doi.101098/rsta.1961.
3. Royal Commission on Environmental Pollution, United Kingdom, 2000, *Energy—The changing climate*, 22nd report, H.M.Stationery Office, London.

Chapter 8
Renewable Sources of Energy

8.1 Introduction

Renewable energy sources may be used directly for heating or indirectly for power (electricity generation), as alternatives to fossil fuels, so they make no call on the world's resources of primary energy. (Combined heat and power is not essentially renewable, rather it is an efficient way of utilising primary energy, and we have discussed it earlier in Chapter 5.)

For heating, in the less-developed countries, forms of renewable energy such as wood, charcoal, and agricultural waste have traditionally been used to meet heating requirements. In developed countries, solar heating (both passive and active) has been used as an alternative to direct or electrical heating, thereby saving fossil fuel use.

For power, much recent discussion has been focussed on renewable electricity generation. The major forms are wind, hydro, geothermal, wave, tidal, wastes and landfill gas, energy crops and, much less so, solar (photovoltaics). Although such sources are large, some virtually infinite, poor economic performance has restricted their implementation until recent years in which state subsidies have been used to encourage their development.

Many of these renewable generation schemes are relatively small scale (e.g., those burning waste or energy crops) and imply distributed electricity generation, small-scale operation near to the demand as opposed to use of very large central power stations. An advantage of distributed generation is that energy is not lost in the distribution system; in a national grid system this can be as much as 10% of the power delivered. But usually the large central power station is more thermally efficient than the smaller non-renewable power station, so there may be less overall advantage in primary energy saving under distributed generation. This is not immediately relevant with small-scale renewable generation in which no primary energy is used anyway (e.g., solar). A national grid may still be essential to provide back-up supplies of electricity when demand is high and the renewable generator is not available for use, perhaps because of adverse weather conditions.

However, there are many large scale hydroelectric power plants, which

107

Table 8.1 Electricity Generated in 2004

Type of Renewable Generation	GWh
Hydro	2,889,094
Municipal waste	47,628
Industrial waste	29,843
Biofuels (liquid)	556
Biogas	20,698
Solid biomass	128,557
Geothermal	55,896
Solar thermal	1,608
Solar photovoltaics	840
Wind	82,259
Tide, waves	551
Total	**3,237,530**

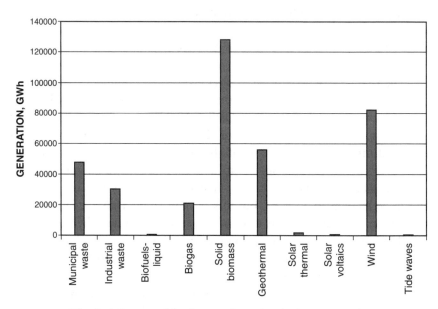

Fig. 8.1. Renewable Generation (GWh) by Source for 2004
Excluding Hydro

Waste, both municipal and industrial, is classified as a renewable primary source. It supplies about 0.28 EJ of electricity generation; again, there is parallel generation of heat from this source, unlisted here.

The fastest growing area of renewable generation is now probably wind power, although somewhat surprisingly the 2004 statistics on this form of electricity generation do not yet reflect a major contribution, only 0.3 EJ, less than 0.5% of worldwide generation. Indeed, these 2004 IEA statistics for wind power are so small that either they are somewhat suspect or growth over the past three years to 2007 (the time of writing) has increased that percentage considerably. There is no associated heat production listed. The worldwide contributions from tidal, waves, and photovoltaics are at present negligible in comparison with other renewables listed before.

We discuss further some of these various forms of renewable power generation separately.

8.3.2 The Renewables Contribution to Primary Energy Supply

The second form of assessment of the contribution of renewables is less readily obtained. As in the first chapter, the contributions to the world primary energy supply may be broken down into the fossil fuel contributions (coal, natural gas, oil, "traditional" renewables, new renewables, and large hydro). For example, the last three were given for 2004 by the IEA as 1.17, 0.04, and 0.24 Gtoe, respectively, with the first of these being mainly through heating rather than generation. Here we can obtain the second and third contributions by working backward from the IEA statistics on generation.

Consider the large hydro contribution of 2.9 million GWh in 2004. To convert this figure into the primary energy saved, we can note that the conversion of GWh to Mtoe is 1 GWh = 8.6×10^{-5} Mtoe, giving $2.9 \cdot 10^{6} \cdot 8.6 \cdot 10^{-5} = 240$ Mtoe or 0.24 Gtoe as listed before. But if we assume this large hydro generation would otherwise have to be supplied by a power station of thermal efficiency 0.38, then the 2.9 million GWh electricity contribution in 2004 would have used 0.24/0.38 = 0.66 Gtoe. (A simpler more direct conversion that British Petroleum uses in presenting their world primary energy contributions notes that 1 Mtoe produces approximately 4,500 GWh in a conventional power station so that the hydro contribution in 2004 would have saved $2.9 \cdot 10^{6} / 4500 = 0.64$ Gtoe, and and this is the figure British Petroleum gives in their presentation of data on the world primary energy supply, comparable to the figure calculated before).

Table 8.2 Contributions to Primary Energy Supply (2005)

Fuel	Contribution, Gtoe
Coal	2.9
Oil	4.0
Natural gas	2.4
Hydro	0.25
Nuclear	0.7
Combustible renewables and waste	1.1
Others including geothermal, solar, wind, heat etc.	0.06
Total	**11. 4**

The various contributions to total primary energy supply given by the IEA for 2005 (rather than the renewable data alone quoted for 2004) are listed in Table 8.2.

Note that here the IEA has not converted the hydro contribution to an equivalent as British Petroleum has done, although they do use such a conversion for nuclear primary energy from electricity generation.

8.4. Types of Renewable Generation

8.4.1 Energy Crops and Biofuels

Fast growing *energy crops*, which are included within solid biomass sources listed before, can be used as a fuel for power generation. They also have the advantage that they can absorb carbon dioxide in their rapid growth and this helps to balance some of the CO_2 that they return to the atmosphere when they burn. But one harvesting and burning of an energy crop has to be followed by another planting cycle for it to qualify as fully renewable.

Energy crops such as coppice and willow can be used too, as fuel to supply power stations, but they are not entirely carbon neutral as they absorb some energy in being transported to the power station where the necessary auxiliary plant may also absorb primary energy. On the world scene relatively few energy crops are yet used for substantial electricity generation mainly because large quantities are required to produce any substantial amount of power.

It should be noted that energy crops (biofuels) are also increasingly used as fuels for transport. For example, bioethanol is a processed fuel developed from fermentation of sugars (the action of micro-organisms such as yeast). The sugars are obtained from sugar cane, maize, cassava, sweet potatoes, and even wood. (The main carbohydrate of these plants is in the form of starch and initial processing is required to produce the sugars.) The required product is ethanol, which is obtained by distillation; it does not substitute directly for petrol but may be used as an "extender" to produce gasohol, which contains some 26% ethanol.

For many years, Brazil has used ethanol in over half its cars but has used a large land area for its production. In 2005, 16.4 billion litres were produced using 2.7 million hectares of land area for this production, some 4.5% of Brazilian land area. Most of this was used as fuel for ethanol-powered vehicles in the domestic market.

Another energy crop is used to produce biodiesel, a diesel-equivalent. This is a processed fuel derived from biological sources. The fuel is obtained by crushing of crops, such as rape, soya beans, or oil palms (but recycled cooking oils can also be used). Biodiesel produces less net carbon dioxide emissions than petroleum-based diesel, but its calorific value is about 10% less. It can be burnt directly in diesel engines but its combustion is then incomplete and this leads to carbon formation in the engine cylinders. Biodiesel is blended with about 95% conventional diesel for transport in the United Kingdom, but higher biodiesel percentages can be used, up to 20%. It can also be used as a heating fuel in domestic and commercial boilers.

While the immediate attractions of these biofuels are obvious, in reducing primary energy demand and carbon dioxide reduction, concern has been expressed about possible overuse of land for the required plant production. Oil palms in particular need warm humid conditions and are largely grown in southeast Asia on land from which rain forest has been cleared. So the reduction in carbon dioxide from use of biodiesel may be balanced out by the loss of these rain forests, which themselves were absorbing CO_2 often on a massive scale.

8.4.2 Waste

As indicated above there are an increasing number of renewable power stations based on *industrial waste and landfill gas*, although they do not yet make a substantial contribution to meet world electricity demand.

The calorific value of the waste is low compared with conventional fuels so the quantities required to meet a particular demand will be relatively large. The efficiency is also relatively low, both the boiler efficiency and the plant thermal efficiency being less than those for a conventional plant, because of lower pressure and temperature levels in the latter. But of course they would produce some greenhouse gases if they simply degenerated, without being used for generation. So while such waste plants undoubtedly reduce the calls on primary fossil fuel resource, they are not entirely carbon free in the production of their exhaust gases, and their classification as fully renewable is open to discussion.

8.4.3 Wind

The growing installation of windmills generating electricity is visible in many countries, but there are pros and cons to windpower. The *advantage* lies in the replacement of a fossil-fueled plant by carbon-free production of electrical power. Not only is a plant using primary fossil fuel resource being replaced, but overall carbon production is being reduced since the new installation produces no carbon dioxide once it is up and running.

The *disadvantages* of windpower are several. The first relates to environmental visual impact; most modern windmills are not small. For example, a plant developing 2 MW may require a rotor of some 70 meters in diameter, spinning about a horizontal axis. Planning regulations have to take account of these environmental aspects; if a new plant is to be located onshore in an area of considerable natural beauty, then local residents will usually be vocal in their objections.

The second lies in the cost of electricity. Although the power supply is for free, the capital costs are large in comparison with those of a conventional plant. For example a capital cost of £1,000 per kilowatt is representative for a land-based wind plant; with a discount factor of 0.1 and an averaged out generating time of say 2,000 hours per year leads the simple analysis of electricity costs given in Appendix A to a generation cost of about 5 p/kWh, to which must be added a maintenance cost.

This is likely to be greater than comparable costs of conventional plants as indicated in Appendix A, so that a developer will require state subsidy or other fiscal encouragement, as indicated earlier. As more windmills are made, so the capital cost per kilowatt will come down, and this will reduce the electricity price. But the problem of relatively low utilisation remains, the wind does not always blow, and this adversely affects the economics in comparison with conventional plants. (We shall return to this question of generating time and power output later).

The third problem of intermittent operation also causes problems for a national grid as discussed in section 8.4.

Environmental objections may be overcome by placing the windmills offshore, but this increases the capital cost because of the electricity connection to the shore, to the national grid and the consumer. But with these disadvantages outlined, wind power remains an attractive option and it is the fastest developing means of renewable generation.

8.4.3.1 Basic Concepts

A short discussion may help us to understand the basic concepts of wind power development. We concentrate on "axial flow" wind turbines or windmills in which the rotor rotates about a horizontal axis.

The mass flow through the turbine is controlled by the wind speed V and is proportional to its frontal area, which for a turbine of diameter D is $\pi D^2/4$. The mass flow is thus $\rho V \pi D^2/4$. The kinetic energy in the wind stream is proportional to $V^2/2$ per unit mass flow, although the turbine does not abstract all of the kinetic energy in the stream.

The amount of power produced (P) is proportional to this specific kinetic energy $V^2/2$, and to the mass flow, so it can be expressed in the form quoted by Taylor (1),

$$P = kV^3 \pi D^2/4 \qquad [8.1]$$

where P is in kWh per year; k is an empirical constant of about 3.2, depending on the characteristics of the turbine and its design.

If we consider the 2 MW (2,000 kW) turbines of 70 metres quoted above (which is the form of one of the Vestas turbines used in the Blyth field off the northeast coast of the United Kingdom) then a check would give an estimate of the rated wind speed V_R, for an operational mean time of, say, 2,000 hours (the equivalent time per year it could be regarded as operating at its full 2 MW rating). From the equation

$$P = kV_R^3 \pi D^2/4, \qquad [8.2]$$

$$2000 \cdot 2000 = 3.2 V_R^3 \pi 70^2/4$$

This equation yields the rated wind speed of $V_R = 6.87$ metres per second. Thus this plant would provide 2 MW for 2,000 hours if it operated continuously for this time in each year at 6.87 m/s. The wind does not blow continuously at this speed all the year so we must look in more detail at what happens.

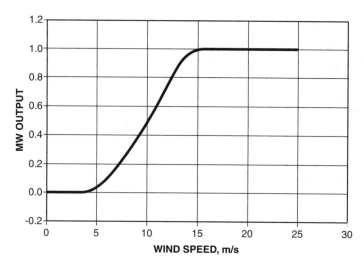

Fig. 8.2. *a,* Power Output Against Wind Speed for a
Typical 1 MW Rated Wind Turbine

8.4.3.2 Wind Energy Distribution

This is an oversimplified calculation, which has used an operational mean time of 2,000 hours per annum, as yet unjustified. But wind power provides a good illustration of intermittency (Taylor [1]) and the operational time may be estimated more reasonably.

First, it has to be appreciated that the power output from a wind turbine varies with the wind speed. The generating plant has to withstand extreme conditions without being destroyed and modern turbines are designed to withstand maximum wind speeds of about 25 m/s at which the turbine is switched off for protection. Figure 8.2a shows an example of the wind power output from a small turbine of maximum output 1 MW. The wind turbine will "cut-in"at a low speed of a few metres per second; there is no wind power below 4–5 m/s, which is a significant constraint. Power then rises steadily up to the rated power at say 15 m/s, and remains at this level up to a speed of perhaps 25 m/s at which the plant is shut down for safety considerations.

The wind speed will vary over the year and a typical turbine will experience so many hours of operation at each speed as Figure 8.2b shows for a hypothetical site. Such a plot may be obtained from experimental observations of the time that the turbine operates in a "band" of wind speed,

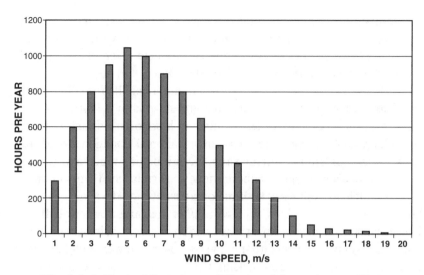

Fig. 8.2. *b,* Typical Spectrum of Hours of Operation per Year
at Various Wind Speeds

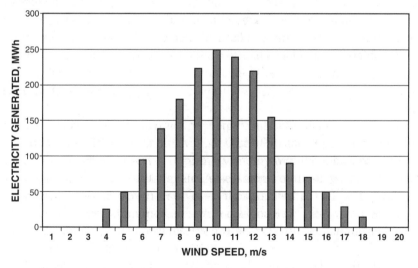

Fig. 8.2. *c,* Electric Power Generated at Various Wind Speeds
by 1 MW Rated Wind Turbine

say, 1.5 to 2.5 m/s giving 600 hours for an average wind speed of 2 metres
per second shown in the graph. Using the two graphs, Figures 8.2*a* and 8.2*b*
together, the power output at each of these various speeds can be obtained as

in Figure 8.2c. The power outputs in each band may be summed to give the total output, in this case 1,835 MWh, and dividing this figure by the number of hours per year (8,760) gives the average output over the year as 0.21 MW for a 1 MW rated turbine on this particular site.

8.4.4 Tidal

Tidal power plants may be introduced in rivers flowing to the sea. Tidal stream schemes simply involve the insertion into the rivers of water turbines, and use the kinetic energy of the tidal flow to provide power, just as windmills use the kinetic energy in air flows. They may be below the surface and if they are relatively small in power output they will cause little disturbance of the river flow and few environmental problems. They are essentially intermittent with a maximum power output at the ebb tide.

Larger schemes, tidal barrages, involve barriers containing the water turbines being placed across the stream. These may restrict some of the maximum outward flow to the sea, enabling water to be stored upstream of the barrier and discharged at a later time. This evens out the power output to some extent, but not entirely, so there are intermittency problems in relation to national grid connections.

Tidal barrages are usually located in large river estuaries and depend directly on the sea's tidal flow. Such a plant is located in France at La Rance and has operated successfully for over forty years developing 240 MW.

One of the biggest tidal schemes proposed is that associated with the Severn barrage in western England. It has been a matter of discussion over many years and no firm commitment has been made to construct it; there have been many environmental objections expressed. An authoritative report by the Severn Tidal Power group in 1989 (2) concluded that a maximum output of 8.64 MW could be achieved with an average power of 2 MW. The capital cost (C) was estimated at about £8 billion on 1989, or some £12 billion in 2006 money, giving a high unit capital cost of £1,390/ kW. It was estimated that this Severn barrage could deliver 17 TWH (about 50 PJ), effectively operating at full load for 2,027 hours per year. A rough estimate of electricity cost based on these figures and using the simplified analysis of Appendix A suggests an electricity cost of 0.7 p/kWh, which is a relatively high electricity price. Clearly the viability of such a scheme depends on the average power output, which is relatively low in comparison with the maximum possible power output, and a major state subsidy would be required for both capital and operation.

8.4.5 Wave Power

Many schemes have been proposed to use sea wave motion to generate electrical power, but for such schemes to make substantial contributions to national power demand they have to extend for very long distances. As with many renewable proposals for generation the substantial capital investment leads to the high electricity price, and there is also the problem of intermittency.

8.4.6 Solar Photovoltaics (PV)

A PV cell consists in essence of a junction between two thin layers of dissimilar semiconducting materials known as p (positive) semiconductors and n (negative) semiconductors. These semiconductors are usually made from crystalline silicon, but the p and n semiconductors are "doped," each with a very small quantity of a different impurity. The n type has a surplus of free electrons and the p type has a deficit of free electrons. A pn junction is formed by joining these dissimilar semiconductors. The essence of the PV cell is that it may generate electricity when light, a stream of photons, falls on it. Power of about 1.5 watts at a voltage of 0.5 volts (i.e., 3 amps) have been obtained,
 This is a simple description of the very complex physics involved in a PV cell. A good description of both the basic physics and the practical development that has been required is given by Boyle (1).
 Solar cells have been used in space applications, and more and more are being used in industrial and commercial buildings. The cells have to be stacked to provide adequate voltage and power and they are very expensive, largely because of the cost of pure silicon. As with other renewable developments (e.g., tidal stream, wave) they have yet to make a substantial contribution to solving world energy resource problems.

8.5 Intermittency

Any discussion of renewable generation must include an assessment of the advantages and disadvantages of distributed generation, which we have mentioned earlier, and the associated problem of intermittency of operation. Instead of a large central power station, many smaller generating plants are used, each nearer to the demand location. (Very often these can be combined heat and power (CHP) plants, which can meet both power and heat demands; then there will be net savings in primary energy.)

An advantage of distributed generation is that energy is not lost in the distribution system; in a national grid this can be as much as 10% of the power delivered, but this has to be balanced against the loss in efficiency associated with use of smaller power stations. However, there is the second problem associated with renewable power production, that of intermittency. This is the variation in power output with time due to natural causes; for example, the variation in wind power output with weather conditions as discussed in section 8.3 or the variation in wave power output with storms and for tidal power with the ebb and flow of tides.

A major problem with renewable generation arises in relation to the fact that renewable power cannot always be called up at the will of the user (or his agent, a national grid). The supply may be intermittent depending on weather; for example, where a high pressure anticyclone hovers over a country in a spell of cold weather there may be virtually no wind for wind turbines and no generated power just when it is needed most. So a national grid is essential to provide back-up supplies of electricity when demand is high and a renewable generator is not available for use.

It can be argued that such backup has to be provided by a national grid anyway, as it has to cope with variations in demand. These are associated not only with adverse weather conditions but also with changes in human behaviour (e.g., the sudden switching on of millions of kettles for a cup of tea when a nation like the United Kingdom takes a halftime break from watching a world cup football match!)

There is yet another problem associated with intermittency that Laughton (3) has pointed out: a basic mismatch between a renewable system of generation and an established national grid. Because renewable generators operate only at low fractions of the hours available in any one year, their installed capacity has to be larger than it would be otherwise in a conventional system in order to meet the demand for electricity. In other words, the ratio of installed renewable power level to the mean power delivered over an annual period is very much larger than the current conventional system. For example, in the example studied in section 8.3, the installed power hypothetical wind turbine was 1 MW but the annual mean power level was only 0.21 MW. There is thus a basic mismatch between such a renewable generating system and the conventional existing grid. (A similar mismatch would arise with the Severn barrage as illustrated before.)

This existing system itself also has a bottleneck through which only a maximum delivery of power can be delivered. For example in the United Kingdom, the maximum demand is in the southeast of the country whereas the major generating system is in the north, the power being delivered through five major north/south main transmission cables. Increased demand in the southeast will have to be met either by building more power stations in that area or by constructing more northern stations coupled with additional north/south main cables. More renewable generation in the north would overload the existing bottleneck, so it could not always be used when renewable power becomes available (much of it in the north, particularly Scotland). A comparable situation has been experienced in Germany where excess wind generation has already met this type of practical engineering constraint.

Thus, there are two intermittency problems associated with intermittent renewable generation: that of power not being available when it is required because of adverse weather conditions, and that of excess power in favourable weather conditions meeting a transmission bottleneck in an existing grid system.

These problems are extremely complex, as Laughton's detailed descriptions and calculations have shown. Studies have been made by the United Kingdom National Grid of the extent to which a national grid such as that in the United Kingdom can cope from the introduction of renewable distributed generation. It was accepted that the existing 10–15% excess installed capacity (the present excess of installed capacity over maximum demand, the so-called grid safety factor) could cope with about 10–15% of distributed generation without substantial requirement for additional electrical plants in the transmission system. But an increase of more than that in renewable and distributed generation would require additional back-up plants and would lead to an increase in the price of electricity making it even more uneconomical requiring even greater subsidy.

8.6 Discussion

It is sometimes argued that renewable resources can supplant fossil fuels and indeed nuclear fuels, there being almost infinite amounts available from the sun. While this is superficially true, there are many difficulties, some economic in terms of the cost of renewable generation largely due to the capital costs rather than the running costs, and others in relation to engineering practicality in matching new renewable systems to established grid systems.

The author has therefore argued elsewhere (4) that while there is a strong case for renewables within the United Kingdom's energy scene it can only be feasible within an energy supply mix.

Such arguments will be considered in more detail in the next chapter where various energy scenarios for the future are discussed.

References

1. Boyle, G. [ed.], 2004, Taylor: Wind energy. Chap. 7 in *Renewable energy*, Oxford University Press, Oxford.
2. Severn Tidal Power, 1989, *The Severn Barrage Project*, General Report, Energy Paper 57, HMSO, London.
3. Laughton, M., 2007, *Renewable energy and the power market bottleneck*, British Management Foundation, London.
4. Rooke, D., Fells, I., and Horlock, J. H. [ed.], 1995, *Energy for the future*, Chapman and Hall, London.

Chapter 9
Energy Scenarios and Energy Policy

9.1 Introduction

In Chapter 1, we considered the energy resources available to the world and the demands being made on those resources in terms of consumption.

The conclusion was that as the world's economies change and expand, so energy demand will grow, with the utilisation of fossil and nuclear fuels increasing unless renewables come into play on a major scale. Subsequently, in later chapters, we considered related environmental factors such as carbon discharge into the atmosphere and the associated global warming.

Here, we discuss some of the complex scenarios that have been drawn to describe the probable energy future. This discussion involves study of the factors which lead to growth in energy consumption and how they may change; the environmental consequences are also described. As the scenarios point out, the consequences are strongly dependent upon mankind's actions in changing these controlling factors.

Scenario predictions are difficult and complex and we do not attempt to carry them out here; rather, we describe the results of some studies made in the recent past. However, the controlling factors are strongly influenced by the energy policies that are adopted by the nations of the world (and their individual populations). The chapter closes with some brief discussion of some of these policies, for the world but more particularly that for one country, the United Kingdom.

9.2 Factors Controlling Energy Consumption and Scenario Predictions

There are several major factors that control world energy consumption. They include population, energy per capita (average energy consumed by individuals), gross domestic product (GDP), energy intensity (defined later), and energy efficiency (related to the way primary energy is used).

Table 9.1 World Population (billions)

Year	1990	2020	2050	2100
Population	5.3	8.1	10.1	12

Source: Davis (1995).

Table 9.2 Primary Energy per Capita (toe) for Various Regions

Area	1960	1990
North America	5.8	7.8
Western Europe	1.8	3.2
Latin America	0.7	1.3
Sub-Saharan Africa	0.4	0.5
South Asia	0.3	0.4
World	1.1	1.7

Source: Davis (1995).

9.2.1 Population and Energy Per Capita

Obviously a major controlling factor is *world population*, its growth and distribution. Table 9.1 shows World Energy Council (WEC) estimates of global population reported by Davis (1) in 1995. In their 1998 studies (which we shall review later) the WEC (2) used figures of 5.3 billion in 1990, 10.1 billion in 2050, and 11.7 in 2100.

Energy per capita is then a factor that relates energy consumption to population, Although this per capita figure is attractive in its simplicity there is a wide disparity in energy availability and energy consumption round the world so there are major variations in the primary energy per capita for different regions. Table 9.2 shows values for different regions given by Davis (1) and how they changed from 1960 to 1990. These wide variations, together with recent marked increases in India and China, mean that estimates of world consumption of primary energy use from this factor, coupled with local population estimates, are difficult to make.

9.2.2 GDP and Energy Intensity

An alternative path to follow in scenario study is to estimate first the GDP of different regions and attempt to project this forward.

If local GDPs can be established then another quantity can be brought into play: the *energy intensity*. This is defined as the amount of energy required to produce a unit of GDP. It increases during the first stage of industrialisation in developing countries but then decreases, as observed in maturing economies. In developed countries the rate of growth in energy consumption is decoupled over time from the rate of growth of GDP, resulting in a decrease of energy intensity. But again, the local variations in GDP and energy intensity estimates are so wide that this method of forward prediction is also difficult.

9.2.3 Energy Efficiency

A final factor with major influence is *energy efficiency*, essentially the way primary energy is used. Energy efficiencies not only affect the sketching out of future scenarios but proposed changes in them (e.g., shifts in transport use, reduced heat losses) have become important features within the definition of national energy policies. We defer discussion of a precise definition of energy efficiency until after a review of some scenarios.

9.3 Energy Scenarios

9.3.1 For the World—The WEC Scenarios

Authoritative work on world scenarios using these various factors has been carried out by the World Energy Council, first in 1993, more recently in 1998, then updated and published in 2000 (2). This work has involved predictions of world population increase, of parallel economic growth, and the way energy is used across the world, and after some up-to-date analysis was reported in a major report (2).

Initially, in 1993, three main scenarios were studied:

1. A case assuming a high rate of economic growth;
2. A reference case, which assumed things would go on much as they were doing at the time of writing; and
3. An "ecologically driven" case, in which the world would make major attempts to reduce its dependence on energy.

The reference case B was then divided into two, with an additional case reflecting stronger growth in energy consumption in developing countries. The results of this round of "scenario" studies by the World Energy Council in 1993 suggested that on the "business as usual basis" the annual demand for primary energy would increase from about 9 Gtoe in 1990 to about 13 Gtoe in 2020. For the high growth case, it would reach 17 Gtoe in 2020; but for the ecologically driven case world energy consumption would be held to about 11 Gtoe in 2020.

These three "families" of scenarios were modified for the 1998 study, which carried predictions forward to 2050 and tentatively even beyond to 2100. Three variations of case A were introduced with different emphases on various fossil fuels. Case B became a single case again but case C was divided, one assuming development in energy efficiency but with nuclear power phased out by 2100 and the other assuming an expanding role for nuclear power.

We shall concentrate here on the 1998/2000 results; the main features of the scenarios are summarised in Table 9.3. The projections for 2050 and 2100 are summarised. Note that the three A cases give the same overall prediction for world consumption as do the two C cases, but the different mix of fuels is indicated in the table.

This different mix is reflected in the very large variations in the predictions of the carbon emissions and in the use of fossil fuel resource indicated in Table 9.3. This may be compared to the estimates of resources made by the WEC in 1993 as reported in Chapter 1, where they were compared with recent BP figures for actual consumption in the period 1990–2004.

More detailed results for the estimated breakdown of primary energy consumption were included in the 1998/2000 report, for 2050 compared with the base year 1990, for all six scenarios of the 1998/2000 study (A1, A2, A3), B, and C (C1, C2). See Table 9.4.

9.3.2 The WEC Conclusions

In its conclusions, the WEC placed emphasis on the growth in carbon emissions; only two of the scenarios showed atmospheric concentrations less than double the preindustrial figure.

The Council also strongly drew attention to the opportunities that exist to save primary energy; over 60% is in effect wasted.

Another chastening comment made in 1998 (the time of presentation of their analyses) was that just over 75% of the world's current primary energy supplies came from fossil fuels, and only 2% from new renewables other than large hydro (although that latter figure has increased in recent years). They added that about one third of the world's population had no access to commercial energy services.

Table 9.3 Major Features from the WEC Scenarios, 1998/2000

	(A) High Growth	(B) Middle Course	(C) Ecologically Driven
Number of Scenarios	3	1	2
Population (billions)			
1990	5.3	5.3	5.3
2050	10.1	10.1	10.1
2100	11.7	11.7	11.7
Primary energy demand, Gtoe			
1990	9	9	9
2050	25	20	14
2100	45	35	21
Resource availability			
Fossil	High	Medium	Low
Nonfossil	High	Medium	Low
CO_2 emission constraint	No	No	Yes (tax)
Carbon emissions, GtC			
1990	6	6	6
2050	9-15	10	5
2100	6-20	11	2

Finally, they added a surprisingly upbeat comment: that "although some may claim that fossil fuel reserves are restricted, the reality is that geological resources for these fuels and uranium are huge and technological advances are allowing more and more of them to be exploited" (2). Finally, the WEC concluded that the decarbonisation of the fuel mix was likely to be a very protracted process.

9.3.3 Regional and National Scenarios

The WEC world scenarios were broken down to give regional predictions (for the OECD countries, the developing countries and those with economies in transition). Some regions and indeed individual countries have drawn their own national scenarios to inform governmental policies; these scenarios can be more localised.

Table 9.4 Primary Energy Consumption Mix.
Further features from the WEC scenarios, 1998/2000

	Base Year, 1990	Scenario A1 2050	Scenario A2 2050	Scenario A3 2050	Scenario B 2050	Scenario C1 2050	Scenario C2 2050
Primary energy (Gtoe total)	9	25	25	25	20	14	14
Fuel mix percent							
Coal	24	15	32	9	21	11	10
Oil	34	32	19	18	20	19	18
Gas	19	19	22	32	23	27	23
Nuclear	5	12	4	11	14	4	12
Renewables	18	22	23	30	22	39	37

9.3.3.1 The RCEP Scenario

One such national prediction has been made by the British Royal Commission on Environmental Pollution (RCEP) (3). Paralleling the WEC work on the world picture, the RCEP introduced four basic scenarios for the United Kingdom aimed at achieving their target of a 60% reduction in CO_2 production by 2050. One was dominantly related to supply modification and two were led by demand modification; a fourth involved major changes in both demand and supply.

The first assumed that 1998 demand would be held to 2050 (a major challenge in itself when viewed against the anticipated growth in gross domestic product [GDP]) and that massive changes would be made in energy supply. In particular, new and renewable energy supplies would increase twentyfold. The nuclear supply would increase fourfold, to 46 times the Sizewell B power station output of 1.2 GW (or that equivalent generation would come from fossil fuel plants with carbon sequestration and storage, so-called CSS plants). A Severn tidal barrage would be built and thousands of combined heat and power plants would be introduced to provide low-grade heat as well as electricity. Electrically driven heat pumps would be widely used. Transport energy demand would increase but the fuel use and CO_2 production would be held back by the use of increasingly efficient vehicles and hydrogen fuel cells (also assumed in the other scenarios). The second and third scenarios were primarily influenced by demand modification (but not entirely). Both were supposed to achieve a 36% reduction in primary energy supply through low-grade heat reduction and through the use of CHP systems. But the assumptions on the supply side were different between these two scenarios. In the second, no nuclear contribution was assumed, but a major expansion of renewable generation (to 45 GW, well over half the current total United Kingdom installed generation capacity) was advocated. In the third scenario, a mix of renewable (wind, wave, and tidal stream), nuclear, and CCS generation was postulated. In total this change in supply was also dramatic, the nuclear component alone corresponding to 19 Sizewell B plants. This emphasis on new electricity generation would enable electricity-driven heat pumps to supply large quantities of low-grade heat.

The fourth scenario postulated a very large reduction in the primary energy used. This would be achieved by

a. A massive modification in demand, by 47% from that of 1997, involving a 70% reduction in low-grade heat requirement, and

b. A 30% reduction in other components of primary energy supply; the shift to renewable generation was not as dramatic as in the other scenarios (no Severn barrage was assumed), but it still involved some 20 GW compared with the base line figure of some 3 GW.

We comment later on the implications and the actions required from the RCEP report, but after consideration of energy efficiency in the next section.

9.4 Energy Efficiency

The citizens of the world are frequently exhorted by their governments to increase energy efficiency in order to solve the twin problems of impending energy shortage and increasing carbon dioxide production (coupled with global warming). Later in this chapter we shall consider various ways in which energy efficiency can be increased and the policies that may be followed to solve these problems.

The term energy efficiency is often loosely used and a tighter definition is required before we consider the ways in which it may be increased. The concepts of thermal efficiency and heating process efficiency (or boiler efficiency) were precisely defined in earlier chapters, each as the ratio of useful energy produced to the primary energy input. Thus the thermal efficiency of a power plant is the ratio of the useful work output (W_U) to the primary fuel energy input (F_E), and the heating process efficiency of a boiler is the ratio of the useful heat produced (Q_U) to the primary fuel energy input (F_B); namely.

$$\eta_{TH} = W_U/F_E, \; \eta_B = Q_U/F_B \qquad [9.1]$$

There are other factors are involved relating to how well we use the useful energy provided to meet our requirements. If our house is poorly insulated, heat (Q_L) is lost to the atmosphere through the walls and windows, so the heat needed to maintain our house at a comfortable temperature (the required heat Q_{REQ}) is less than the useful heat received from the boiler. In addition, an amount of heat may come in for free (say that received from passive solar heating, Q_F). Thus the useful heat and the required heat are related by

$$Q_U = Q_{REQ} + Q_L - Q_F \qquad [9.2]$$

A similar analysis may relate to the use of the electrical work supplied. If electrical equipment remains switched on when it is not being used, say overnight, then some of the electricity delivered to our house is wasted. Failure to install low-wattage lightbulbs means that delivered electricity is also wasted. So there is another effective loss, work that is supplied but not used properly, say W_L, and if the basic electrical work required is W_{REQ}, then

$$W_U = W_{REQ} + W_L \qquad [9.3]$$

From these four equations it follows that the total primary energy supplied is

$$F = F_E + F_B = (W_U/\eta_{TH}) + (Q_U/\eta_B)$$

$$= [(W_{REQ} + W_L)/\eta_{TH}] + [(Q_{REQ} + Q_L - Q_F)/\eta_B]. \qquad [9.4]$$

An overall energy efficiency can be defined for the house (η_{EE}) as the ratio of the energy requirement to the primary energy used

$$\eta_{EE} = (W_{REQ} + Q_{REQ})/F$$

and this can be expressed as

$$\eta_{EE} = (W_{REQ} + Q_{REQ})/\{[(W_{REQ} + W_L)/\eta_{TH}] + [(Q_{REQ} + Q_L - Q_F)/\eta_B]\} \quad [9.5]$$

which is a complicated expression. However, it is clear that the energy efficiency can be maximised by

a. Increasing the efficiencies η_{TH} and η_B,
b. Reducing the losses W_L and Q_L, and
c. Maximising the free heat Q_F.

Another way of stating the energy efficiency is by invoking an utilisation factor, the ratio of the required heat and electrical work to the actual quantity supplied,

$$(UF) = (W_{REQ} + Q_{REQ})/(W_U + Q_U). \quad [9.6]$$

Then the energy efficiency becomes

$$\eta_{EE} = (UF)(W_U + Q_U)/[(W_U/\eta_{TH}) + (Q_U/\eta_B)] \quad [9.7]$$

Clearly the objective must be to increase both the utilisation factor (UF) and the plant efficiencies η_{TH} and η_B.

This simple analysis illustrates the complexity of defining energy efficiency for a single residence. Using the concept at a national level becomes even more complex.

As the World Energy Council pointed out in presenting its various energy scenarios, there is huge scope to raise energy efficiencies—both the efficiencies with which energy is provided (η_{TH} and η_B) and the effectiveness of its utilisation (UF). Over 60% of primary energy is, in effect, wasted, and much of that by end users.

9.5 Reduction of Primary Energy Demand by Increasing Energy Efficiency

In this main section, we discuss possible actions to alleviate the problems of fuel consumption and carbon emissions, that is, the practicality of achieving the objectives of energy scenarios such as those outlined in section 9.3. In particular, the position of one developed country, the United Kingdom, is considered in detail. The scenario work of the United Kingdom Royal Commission on Environmental Pollution (RCEP) is examined in order to list possible actions that would lead to the required substantial savings. The long term objective of the RCEP was a 60% reduction in carbon emissions by 2050. Fells and Horlock (4) emphasised the enormity of this task and proposed a "half-way house" in which the best existing technology could be used to get started on the long term objective of the RCEP. This approach is outlined in section 9.5.1.

As illustrated in the last section, the overall energy efficiency of an individual household or other establishment can be increased by higher energy utilisation factors. On the heating side, this can be done by improving the insulation of existing buildings, by designing new ones with better conservation and by using solar heating, passive or active, to gain free heat. Increase of the "electrical" utilisation factor can also be achieved by using more efficient electrical appliances such as long-life electric lightbulbs, which provide the required light intensity with less electricity, and by switching off our appliances when they are not in use. But in parallel increases in the boiler efficiencies of heating devices and the thermal efficiencies of power stations must also be sought.

On the national scene, there can be improvements in the efficiencies of domestic and commercial heaters, usually boilers, and industrial heating processes. Modern condensing boilers are now being installed in many houses and office blocks in the United Kingdom. Heat is lost in boiler flue gases if they contain water vapour; in the new boilers, these gases are condensed and the heat saved is recirculated within the boiler. This increases boiler efficiency from some 60–70% to some 90%, and for a given output will save the gas or oil input (and the heating bills). Similarly, there is great scope for increasing the heating efficiency of many industrial processes.

Thermal efficiencies may be raised nationally, for example, by replacing coal-fired power plants of low thermal efficiency (some 35–40%) with combined cycle gas-fired turbine plants (of some 55–60% thermal efficiency). This has the additional benefit of reducing the carbon dioxide production.

In the area of transport, there is similar scope for energy saving in two ways: through increasing power plant efficiencies and utilisation factors. Higher efficiency internal combustion engines result from improved technical design and lead to better fuel consumption, more miles to the gallon or a lower figure of litres per kilometre. Higher utilisation factors can be obtained in various ways. For example, higher fuel consumption arises during urban driving when the engine operates "off-design," so the less time spent idling in traffic the better. New hybrid cars now enable the car to be driven by battery power in the idling condition, the batteries being charged during more efficient operation at higher road speeds. Excessive speeds also lead to higher fuel consumption, so keeping speed down to an optimum level can save fuel. Thus, the whole national driving pattern influences both the mean thermal efficiency and the utilisation factor, leading to higher overall energy efficiency.

9.5.1 Magnitudes of Possible Savings from Increasing Energy Efficiency: The Example of the United Kingdom

9.5.1.1 Heating Processes

In the area of energy use in heating processes there is scope for major savings by increases in energy efficiency. The use of simple, relatively low-grade technologies, which are immediately available, offer marked benefits in energy efficiency, and they do not have the adverse economic effect of small investments in capital resulting in major savings in running costs. These simple technologies include:

a. Improved building insulation,
b. Small-scale solar heating, particularly for domestic hot water,
c. Small- and medium-sized combined heat and power plants (CHP), for industrial use, hospitals, blocks of flats, supermarkets, public buildings and
d. Heat pumps, for uses similar to those in *c.*

We can illustrate the possible savings that could be achieved in a developed country from increases in energy efficiency by reference to an energy review written by the Performance and Innovation Unit (the PIU) for the United Kingdom government in 2002 (5).

The overall primary energy demand in the United Kingdom for the year 2000 was some 220 million tonnes of oil equivalent (Mtoe) from which about 149 millions tonnes of carbon emissions (MtC) were produced. Of this amount of carbon pollution, no less than 71 MtC came from heat loads in the domestic, services, and industry sectors.

"Simple" technology can be used to make reductions in the carbon production from the national heat load. The PIU made an excellent assessment of the potential annual energy savings in the domestic services and industrial sectors that could come from application of these simple technologies to increase energy efficiency over a ten-year period.

It was assumed that in the domestic sector required comfort standards would not change significantly so the internal heat demand (Q_{REQ}) would essentially be unchanged. But reductions in primary energy should be achieved mainly by use of improved building insulation, more efficient domestic boilers, subsidised solar heating of domestic hot water, and heat recovery from air-conditioning systems. Similarly, these low-level technologies could be used in the services sector.

In the industrial sector, the PIU argued that there should be opportunity for the use of more capital intensive and sophisticated technologies, for example, CHP and heat pumps, particularly for reasonably large units. For example, if some 3–5 GW of existing large-scale electricity generation were replaced by locally distributed generation CHP, the carbon reduction comes almost "for free." The replacement of the central power station generation by local, less thermodynamically efficient distributed CHP stations would indeed require a higher fuel input overall. This should be greatly outweighed by the fact that whereas the heat formerly rejected by the big stations is lost, the "rejected" heat from the small CHP stations (somewhat greater than the assumed 3–5 GW of electrical output) would be utilised. This saves the equivalent boiler fuel in the heating devices to be discarded.

The PIU made detailed analyses of the economically possible savings in the heat load area, and argued that about half of these should be possible by 2010. If it is argued that all the economically possible PIU savings could come through by 2025, then about 17 Mtoe would be saved in the domestic sector, 4 Mtoe in the services sector, and 9 Mtoe in the industrial sector—a total of some 30 Mtoe—nearly 14% of the United Kingdom's primary energy use in 2000.

The corresponding carbon savings depend on the mix of fuels used in the heating area, and the nature of the various technologies used for savings. Ratios of carbon savings to energy savings (MtC/Mtoe) corresponding to different fuels are about 0.63 for gas, 0.85 for oil, and 1.08 for coal; all for assumed complete combustion to CO_2. Taking a mean ratio of 0.8 MtC/mtoe, the economically possible carbon savings in the heat load area should be of the order of 24 MtC by 2025 (the Fells and Horlock target date), that is, some 16% of the 149 MtC produced in the United Kingdom in 2000.

9.5.1.2 Electricity Generation

Parallel savings in primary fuel energy should be possible by increases in the thermal efficiency of electricity generation together with reduction of carbon. The PIU suggested that for the United Kingdom it should be possible to meet 18% of the country's generation from renewable sources (primarily wind power) and that this should be enough to meet the increased demand for electricity over the period. Fells et al. (4) accepted this point but argued for other substantial carbon savings by more substantial actions, but using available technology.

They proposed replacing existing coal-fired plants (which produced 27 MtC in 2000) with

a. New coal plants employing carbon sequestration and storage (CSS) and
b. A major tidal generation scheme.

The first of these schemes (CSS, as described in Chapter 3) would not contribute to reduction in primary energy consumption, but would reduce carbon discharge into the atmosphere as some 85% of the carbon dioxide produced would be separated out, liquefied, and stored under the North Sea. It was estimated that 8 MtC would be saved in this way. The second would replace another one third of coal-fired generation leading to carbon savings saving of the order of 5 MtC.

Thus, a savings of 24 MtC come from heat load changes and a further 13 MtC from electricity generation. Following and developing the PIU work, Fells and colleagues (4) considered that a total reduction of 37 MtC should be possible by 2025, some 25% of the United Kingdom's production of carbon in 2000 (149 MtC). They assumed that nuclear generation would continue at the 2000 level (by replacement of some current plants coming to an end of their safe lives) and that increases in the thermal efficiency of transport power plants would hold carbon production in the transport sector (they saw little hope of reduction in use of cars and larger vehicles).

The Fells and Horlock (F/H) proposal for improvements in energy efficiency in the United Kingdom would lead to a reduction of 25% in carbon emission by 2025, compared with the RCEP scenario of 60% for 2050. It is clear that the F/H proposal would be but a modest step on the way to the RCEP objective, which has now been taken onboard by the United Kingdom. government. Fells and Horlock argued that these could be achieved with simple technology and with engineering developments, which are feasible now or very soon, practical and achievable steps by 2025 to set the country on its way to more ambitious target for 2050.

A possible practical scheme has been described for increasing energy efficiency to reduce primary energy demand and carbon production in one country. Many others are being proposed for other countries and regions (e.g., the European Union).

9.6 The World Scene—Possible Savings

Implementation of a world scenario such as one of those described earlier is a daunting task. Many writers have emphasised the enormity of the problem. Rather than review all of these comments here we concentrate on a challenging approach adopted by the Princeton University environmental research group, notably Socolow and Pascala (6).

9.6.1 The Princeton "Wedge" Concepts

The work described in Chapter 7 on carbon emissions by Socolow, Lam, Pascala and others at Princeton led that group to propose a number of drastic actions that would be required if carbon emissions were to be contained and global warming restricted.

Figure 3.13 showed the Princeton proposal for beginning to restrict carbon emissions immediately. Seven stabilisation "wedges" would be introduced between the "business as usual" and the "holding" line at 7 GtC p.a.; each wedge would involve reaching a reduction of 1 GtC per year over the next fifty years. Assuming linear growth the total avoided emissions per wedge is 25 GtC so the total area of the stabilisation triangle, made up of seven such wedges, would be 175 GtC over the next fifty years.

The enormity of the task before the world is illustrated by Socolow and Pascala (6) who listed fifteen options from which the seven stabilisation wedges could be taken (in fact they would not be separate actions but would interact, more than seven being required to achieve the final objective). The Pascala/Socolow list is shown in abbreviated form in Table 9.5.

Each of these wedge actions is drastic and seven of them (or the equivalent) are required in order to achieve stabilisation of carbon production. Just as the Fells/Horlock proposals for the United Kingdom had to continue beyond 2025, so the Princeton world actions have to continue beyond 2056 and well into the twenty-second century.

9.7 Discussion and Conclusions

Attempts have been made in this chapter to emphasise the enormous problems that have to be overcome to achieve stabilisation of carbon emissions

Table 9.5 The Princeton Wedges

Option	Required Action
1. Efficient vehicles	Increase fuel economy for 2 billion cars from 30 to 60 miles per gallon
2. Reduced use of vehicles	Decrease travel for 2 billion 30 mpg cars from 10,000 miles to 5,000 miles
3. Energy efficient buildings and appliances	Cut electricity use by one quarter
4. More efficient coal power plants	Increase coal power plant efficiency to 60% efficiency instead of 40%
5. Replace coal power plants with gas	Replace 1,400 GW coal plants with gas fired plants
6. Carbon capture at baseload plants	CCS at 800 GW coal plants or at 1600 GW gasified plants
7. Capture CO_2 at H_2 plant	CCS at plants producing 250 Mt H_2/year from coal or 500 Mt H_2 from natural gas plants
8. Capture CO_2 at coal to synfuel plants	CCS at synfuel plants producing 30 million barrels a day from coal
9. Nuclear power for coal power	Add 700 GW nuclear (twice current level)
10. Wind power for coal power	2 million 1MW windmills
11. Photovoltaic for coal power	Add 2000 GW-peak PV (700 times present capacity)
12. Wind-produced H_2 for use in fuel cell cars for gasoline in hybrid car	Add 4 million 1 MW windmills
13. Biomass for fossil fuel	Add 100 times Brazil ethanol production (uses one sixth of world cropland)
14. Reduce deforestation, start new forests and plantations	Decrease tropical deforestation to zero cf current 0.5 GtC/year
15. Conservation tillage	Apply to all cropland, avoiding carbon loss in ploughing after deforestation

and to hold back global warming. The magnitude of the whole problem of climate change, together with the likely economic impact, were emphasised in a substantial report by Sir Nicholas Stern for the United Kingdom government late in 2006 (7). A summary of his major findings form a useful closure to this final chapter.

9.7.1 The Stern Report

9.7.1.1 The Dangers

Stern first reviews the dangers resulting from climate change, noting that all countries will be affected, but that the poorest countries will suffer earliest and most. Average world temperatures could rise by 5°C from preindustrial levels if climate change goes unchecked. Warming of 3 or 4°C will result in many millions more people being flooded and, by the middle of the century, some 200 million people may be permanently displaced due to rising sea levels, heavier floods, and drought. Such warming is likely seriously to affect global food production.

Stern describes the position on greenhouse gases in the atmosphere that has been discussed in Chapter 7—that before the industrial revolution the concentration of CO_2 was 280 parts per million (ppmv) but the current level is some 400 ppmv. He proposes that the level should be limited to 450–550 ppmv, anything higher substantially increasing the risk of very harmful impacts.

9.7.1.2 Recommended Actions

Three elements of policy are required for an effective response: carbon pricing, technology policy, and energy efficiency.

Carbon pricing, through taxation, emissions trading or regulation, will show people the full social costs of their actions. The aim should be a global carbon price across countries and sectors. Emissions trading schemes, like that operating across the European Union, should be expanded and linked.

Technology policy should drive the large-scale development and use of a range of low-carbon and high-efficiency products. Globally, support for energy research and development should at least double; in particular, support for the deployment of low-carbon technologies should increase by up to five times.

Energy efficiency: As we have discussed at length earlier in this chapter, increased energy efficiency is a key factor in solving the climate change problem.

Stern also notes the major effects of *deforestation,* which are responsible for more emissions than the transport sector. He therefore suggests that large-scale international pilot programmes should be introduced to explore the best ways to curb deforestation and that they should be started very quickly. International funding should also go into researching new crop varieties that will be more resilient to drought and flood.

More generally, he proposes that climate change should be fully integrated into development policy, and rich countries should honour pledges to increase support through overseas development assistance. International funding should support improved regional information on climate change impacts.

9.7.1.3 Economic Impacts

Many people have made most of these points before, but the major original impact of Stern's work has come through his studies of the coupling between climate change and world economics. He points out that unabated climate change could cost the world at least 5% of gross domestic product (GDP) each year; but if more dramatic predictions come to pass, that cost could be more than 20% of GDP.

He emphasises that the benefits of strong, early action would considerably outweigh the costs. For example, each tonne of CO_2 we emit causes damage worth at least $85, but reduced emissions could be achieved at a cost of less than $25 a tonne.

Stern considers that the cost of reducing emissions could be limited to around 1% of global gross domestic product (GDP). Further, shifting the world onto a low-carbon path could eventually benefit the world economy by $2.5 trillion a year. He notes that by 2050 markets for low-carbon technologies could be worth at least $500 billion.

He emphasises the benefits of early action on longer-term world prospects. What we do now can have only a limited effect on the climate over the next 40 or 50 years, but what we do in the next 10–20 years can have a profound effect on the climate in the second half of this century.

9.7.2 Conclusions

Stabilisation of carbon emissions and eventually holding back of global warming will require that very large changes in life style and technology use have to be undertaken. While the small-scale local actions being discussed within western countries are creditable, it is moves on the scale of those listed in the Princeton wedge table that have to be adopted to produce the really major and necessary actions. The Stern report re-emphasises these scientific and technological points but adds that the economic cost of the necessary actions need not be excessive, as long as early action is taken.

References

1. Davis, D. A., 1995, Growth in energy demand and resources. Chap. 1 in *Energy for the future*, edited by Rooke, D., Fells, I., and Horlock, J. H., Chapman and Hall, London.
2. World Energy Council, 2000, *Energy for tomorrow's world—Acting now*, London.
3. Royal Commission on Environmental Pollution, 2000, *Energy—The changing climate*, 22nd report, H.M. Stationery Office, London.
4. Fells, I., Fells, A., and Horlock, J. H., 2005, Cutting greenhouse gas emissions. A pragmatic view, *The Chemical Engineer, July.* *
5. Cabinet Office, 2002, Performance and Innovation Report, United Kingdom Government. *The Energy Review*, February.
6. Socolow, R. H., and Pascala, S. W. 2005, A plan to keep carbon in check, *Scientific American*, September, 1–7.
7. Stern, N., 2006, *the economics of climate change—The Stern Review*. H M Treasury, United Kingdom Government, October.

---

* A more fully developed programme for reducing greenhouse gas emissions, amplifying the original Fells/Horlock proposals of 2005, has since been proposed by Fells and Whitmill in 2008. This is described in a major report published by Fells and associates entitled "A Pragmatic Energy Policy for the UK", and is available on the web site for fells.associates. The report includes a detailed study of the potential of the Severn Barrage.

Appendix A
Economics of Power Plants

A.1 Introduction

The simplest way of assessing the economics of a new power plant is to calculate the unit price of electricity produced by the plant (e.g., in dollars per kilowatt hour) and compare it with that from a conventional plant. This is the method adopted by many authors (1,2). Other methods involving net present values may be used (3,4).

A.2 Electricity Pricing

The method is based on relating electricity price to both the capital related cost and the recurrent cost of production (fuel and maintenance of plant):

$$P_E = \beta C_0 + M + (OM) \qquad [A.1]$$

where
P_E is the annual cost of the electricity produced (e.g. $ per annum); C_0 is the capital cost of plant (e.g., $); $\beta(i, N)$ is a capital charge factor, which is related to the discount rate (i) on capital and the life of the plant (N year) (see section A.3); M is the annual cost of fuel supplied (e.g., $ per annum); (OM) is the annual cost of operation and maintenance (e.g., $ per annum)

The unitised production cost (say $ per kilowatt hour) for the plant is

$$Y_E = \frac{P_E}{\dot{W}H} = \frac{\beta C_0}{\dot{W}H} + \frac{M}{\dot{W}H} + \frac{(OM)}{\dot{W}H} \qquad [A.2]$$

where $\dot{W}$ is the rating of the plant (kW) and H is the plant utilisation (hours per annum).

The cost of the fuel per annum, M, may be written as the product of the

141

unit cost of fuel (ζ,$/kWh) the rate of supply of energy in the fuel ($\dot{F}$,kW) and the utilisation, H, that is,

$$M = \zeta \dot{F} H. \qquad [A.3]$$

Thus, the unitised production cost is then

$$Y_E = \frac{P_E}{\dot{W}H} = \frac{\beta C_0}{\dot{W}H} + \frac{\zeta FH}{\dot{W}H} + \frac{(OM)}{\dot{W}H}$$

$$= \frac{\beta C_0}{\dot{W}H} + \frac{\zeta}{(\eta_0)} + \frac{(OM)}{\dot{W}H} \qquad [A.4]$$

where $\eta_0 = \dfrac{\dot{W}}{\dot{F}}$ is the overall efficiency of the plant. Alternatively the unit

cost of fuel ζ may be written as the cost per unit mass S (say $/kg) divided by the calorific value $[CV]_0$ (kWh/kg}, so that

$$Y_E = \frac{\beta C_0}{\dot{W}H} + \frac{S}{[CV]_0 (\eta_0)} + \frac{(OM)}{\dot{W}H} \qquad [A.5]$$

In the comparison between two competitive plants one may have higher efficiency (and hence, lower fuel cost), but it may have higher capital and maintenance costs. These effects have to be balanced against each other in the assessment of the relative economic merits of two plants.

A.3 The Capital Charge Factor

The capital charge factor (β) multiplied by the capital cost of the plant (C_0) gives the cost of servicing the capital required. Suppose the capital costs of a plant at the beginning of the first year is C_0 and the plant has a life of N years. An annual amount must be provided, which is $[C_0 i + B]$. The first term ($C_0 i$) is the simple interest payment and the second (B) matures into the capital repayment after N years (i.e., interest is added to the accumulated sum at the end of each year); thus

$$B[1 + (1 + i) + (1 + i)^2 + \dots + (1 + i)^{N-1}] = C_0,$$

so that

$$B = \frac{C_0 i}{(1 + i)^N - 1},$$ [A.6]

where it has been assumed that the annual payments are made at the end of each year.

Hence, the total annual payment is

$$C_0 i + B = C_0 \left[i + \frac{i}{(1 + i)^N - 1} \right]$$

$$= C_0 i \left[\frac{(1 + i)^N}{(1 + i)^N - 1} \right]$$ [A.7]

$$= C_0 \beta$$

where the capital charge factor $\beta = \left[\frac{i(1 + i)^N}{(1 + i)^N - 1} \right]$ is sometimes referred

to as the annuity present worth factor.

In arriving at an appropriate value of β, the choice of interest or discount rate (i) is crucial. It depends on:

a.   The relative values of equity and debt financing;
b.   Whether the debt financing is less than the life of the plant;
c.   Tax rates and tax allowances (which vary from one country to another); and
d.   Inflation rates.

In comparing two engineering projects the practice is often to use a test discount rate, applicable to both projects.

A.4 Example of the Use of the Analysis

In the unit price of electricity (Y_E) derived before, the dominant factors are the capital cost per kilowatt ($C_0/\dot{W}$), which generally decreases inversely as the square root of the power (i.e., as $\dot{W}^{1/2}$), the fuel price ζ, the overall efficiency η_0, the utilisation (H hours per year) and to a lesser extent the operational and maintenance costs (OM). Figure 3.14 shows simply how

Y_E, less the (OM/WH) component, varies with $C_0/\dot{W}$ and η_0, for $H = 4,000$ hours and $\zeta = 1$ c/kWh.

Horlock (4) has used this type of chart to compare three lines of development in gas turbine power generation and such examples of electricity pricing are given in the main text in Chapter 3. The basic method is also used to study the pricing of electricity from CHP plants (Chapter 6) and the effects of a carbon tax (Chapter 7).

References

1. Williams, R. H., 1978, Industrial cogeneration, *Ann. Review Energy*, 3, 313–356.
2. Wunsch, A., 1985, Highest efficiencies possible by converting gas turbine plants, *Brown Boveri Review*, 1, 455–456.
3. Horlock, J. H., 1997, *Cogeneration—Combined heat and power plants*, 2nd ed., Pergamon, Oxford.
4. Horlock, J. H., 1997, Aero-engine derivative gas turbines for power generation: Thermodynamic and economic perspectives, *ASME Journal of Engineering for Gas Turbines and Power*, 119, 1, 119–123.

Appendix B
Socolow and Lam Analysis

In Chapter 7 an approximation was given between the annual emission of carbon E in GtC, and the concentration of carbon dioxide in the atmosphere, C,

$$dC/dt = kE, \qquad [B.1]$$

where k is a constant of the order of one half.

Here we review in simple form some analyses by the Princeton climate research group (1), which leads to this approximation.

Consider an approximation to the carbon cycle sketched originally in Figure 7.2. It is supposed that the annual supply of carbon from fossil fuel sources $E(t)$ enters the atmospheric "tank," which has a content C, that some carbon is retained but some moves through to the next tank with content B, representing the biosphere/shallow ocean, and some moves further on to a final tank with content D, representing the deep oceans. Then we can describe the overall carbon flow as follows,

$$\frac{dC}{dt} = -\frac{C-B}{\tau_S} + E \qquad [B.2]$$

$$\beta \frac{dC}{dt} = \frac{(C-B)}{\tau_S} - \frac{(B-D)}{\tau_L} \qquad [B.3]$$

$$\gamma \frac{dC}{dt} = \frac{(C-B)}{\tau_L} \qquad [B.4]$$

These equations contain four parameters τ_S, τ_L, β, and γ. τ_S is a short time constant whereas τ_L is a long time constant; together they control the rate at which the carbon moves between the tanks, and their relative sizes are reflected in Figure AppB.1. β and γ are dimensionless constants, which reflect the capacity of each tank to store carbon, normalised to that of tank C.

145

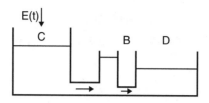

Figure App. B.1

Adding together equations (B.2) and (B.3) then gives

$$\frac{d}{dt}(C + \beta B) = E - \frac{(B - D)}{\tau_L}$$ [B.5]

B.1 The Two-Tank Model

When the supply of carbon is steady, it can be expected that C and B will approach equilibrium and the drain off to D will proceed very slowly, Approximating B by C then yields equations

$$\frac{dC}{dt} = \kappa[E - \frac{C - D}{\tau_L}]$$ [B.6]

$$\frac{dD}{dt} = \frac{1}{\gamma}\frac{C - D}{\tau_L}$$ [B.7]

where $\kappa = 1/(1 + \beta)$. Thus, if γ is very large—the deep oceans have infinite capacity—then the second of these equations shows that D remains virtually constant. The first equation (B.6) then approximates to the very approximate relationship (B.1) as quoted in Chapter 7 where the constant of proportionality k is slightly greater than one half.

References

1.   Socolow, R. H., and Lam, H., 2007, Good enough tools for global warming policy making, *Phil. Trans Royal Society A*, doi.101098/rsta.1961.

Index

A

absolute pressure, 22
absolute temperature scale, 23
absolute" temperature, 21
absorption cycle, 64
acid rain, 91
active solar, 20, 109
active solar heating, 10
adiabatic, 36
aero-engine derivative simple cycle gas turbine, 51
AFBC atmospheric fluidised bed combustion, 57
agricultural and forest wastes, 53
air conditioning, 64
air standard cycles, 81
air standard Joule-Brayton cycle, 38
air standard steady flow cycle, 50
annual cost of electricity produced, 141
annual cost of fuel supplied, 141
annual cost of operation and maintenance, 141
annual emission of carbon, 145
annual supply of carbon from fossil fuels, 92
annual utilisation, 141
automotive transport, 80

B

back pressure steam turbine, 68, 72

basic concepts (wind power), 115
basic IGCC Plant, 45
biodiesel (blended with conventional diesel), 113
bioethanol, 113
biofuels, 112
biomass, 9, 108
biosphere/shallow ocean, 93
boiler, 56, 27
boiler efficiency, 34
boilers and furnaces, 54
bound chemical energy, 1, 19
British Petroleum (BP)
BP Annual Statistics, 5
brake efficiency, 86
brake mean effective pressure, 87
brake power, 87
Brazil (use of ethanol), 113
building insulation, 132
business as usual, 13, 126
by pass engine, 90

C

calculation of real steam plant efficiency, 36
calorific value, 29
calorific value measurement, 30
capital charge factor, 142
capital cost of plant, 142
capital cost per kilowatt *($/W)*, 142
carbon cycle, 93
carbon dioxide, 14

147

carbon dioxide concentration, 94
carbon dioxide production, 92, 96
carbon dioxide tax, 100
carbon emissions, 15, 95, 102
carbon off-setting, 102
carbon pollution, 99
carbon pricing, 100
carbon reduction, 99
carbon reservoirs, 93
carbon sequestration and storage
    (CCS), 135
carbon sequestration and storage
    plant (CCS), 103
carbon trading, 100, 102
CCGT combined cycle gas turbine,
    43
CCGT/back pressure plant, 73
CCGT/pass-out or extraction plant,
    79
CFBC circulatory fluidised beds,
    57
chemical energy, 24
Chinese coal production, 101
Chinese electricity generation, 101
CHP (combined heat and power),
    67
CHP plants, 70, 76
CIS (Commonwealth of Indepen-
    dent States), 12
Clausius, 21
Closed cycle gas turbine plant, 38
cloud formation, 93
coal, 12, 55, 91, 92
coal fired power stations, 98
coefficient of performance (heat
    pump), 60
coefficient of performance (refrig-
    erator), 63
cogeneration plant, 67
combined cycle efficiency, 43

combined cycle gas turbine
    (CCGT), 32, 43, 69
combined gas turbine/steam turbine
    CHP plant, 67
combined heat and power (CHP),
    31, 67
combined heat and power (CHP)
    plants, 32, 53, 67, 98, 129, 134
combustion chamber, 37
commercial sector heating, 59
Commonwealth of Independent
    States, 12
comparison of real IC engine
    performance with air standard
    cycles, 86
comparison of two CHP plants, 73
compression reversible and adia-
    batic, 39
compression stroke, 81
compression-injection (CI) engine,
    80
compressor, 37
concentration of carbon dioxide in
    atmosphere, 15, 94
condensation of flue gases, 62
condensing boiler, 61
constant volume combustion, 24
constant volume gas thermometer,
    23
control surface, 26
conversion table, 3
coppice and willow, 112
corollary of the Second Law, 21
cost of electricity (from windmills),
    114
cost of electricity produced, 50
cost of reducing emissions, 139
coupling between climate change
    and world economics, 139
crude oil, 8

crystalline silicon, 119
CS control surface, 25
CSS carbon sequestration and
    storage, 135
cycle, 20
cycle efficiency, 23
cyclic heat engine, 23
cylinder cooling, 82, 87

D

dangers (from climate change), 139
deep oceans, 145
definitions of efficiency, 28
deforestation, 139
demand modification scenario, 125
development policy (climate
    change), 139
Diesel air standard cycle, 83
Diesel engine/waste heat boiler, 68
dissociation effects, 87
distillation, 4
distributed electricity generation,
    16, 120
distribution of resources, 11, 13
district heating, 25
domestic heating, 55, 59
drag, 88
dual air standard cycle, 84

E

ecological scenarios, 15
ecologically driven case, 125
economics of CHP plants, 73
economics of power plants, 141
economiser, 56
efficiency of Diesel cycle, 83
efficiency of steady flow cyclic
    heat engine, 28
electrical grids, 33
electrical power, 33

electrical work, 2, 19
electricity cost (Severn barrage),
    118
electricity generated, 5, 134
electrolux refrigeration cycle, 64
elementary power plant, 25
emissions regulations, 139
emissions trading, 158
energy, 1
energy consumption (world), 123
energy crops and biofuels, 112
energy crops for transport, 112
energy demand for heating, 18
energy efficiency, 125, 129
energy future, 123
energy intensity, 124
energy per capita, 124
energy policies, 123
energy resources, 17
energy saving (transport), 132
energy scenarios, 123, 125
energy utilisation factor (EUF), 73,
    132
engine thrust, 88
enthalpy, 26
environmental factor, 14
ethanol, 113
EUF Energy Utilisation Factor, 70
European agreement, 92
European countries, 98
European Union, 78
exajoule, 2
exhaust stroke, 81

F

fast breeder reactors, 47
fast reactor, 47
Fells and Horlock, 132,
final nozzle, 88
fired HRSG, 72

First Law, 20
fiscal measures, 100
flow work, 26
fluidised bed combustion (FBC)
    boilers, 57
force, 1
fossil fuel, 5
fossil fuel reserves, 13
four stroke power plant, 80
free heat, 130
fuel cell, 48
fuel cost per unit mass, 50
fuel oils, 98
furnace efficiency, 59
furnaces, 54
fusion, 48

G

gas cooled ractors, 48
gas fired combined cycle plants, 43
gas turbine, 37
gas turbine (or Diesel engine) /
    waste heat boiler, 69
gas turbine internal combustion
    plant, 37
gas turbine power generation costs,
    144
gas turbine with waste heat boiler,
    72
gasohol, 113
gauge pressure, 22
geothermal heat, 10
gigatonne, 2
global GDP, 125
global temperatures, 97
global warming, 14, 91
gross domestic product (GDP), 125
Gore, Senator Al, 96
government subsidy (wind power),
    114

grate boilers, 57
greenhouse gases, 92
grid safety factor, 127
gross domestic product (GNP), 125
gigatonnes of oil equivalent (Gtoe),
    2

H

heat, 1, 19
heat loss, 130
heat pumps, 60
heat recovery from the flue gases,
    58
heat recovery steam generator
    (HRSG), 62, 72
heat to work ratio, 67, 73
heating and refrigeration processes,
    53
heating devices, 54
heating process (boiler) efficiency,
    34
heating processes (savings), 133
heavy-duty CCGT plant, 51
heavy-duty simple cycle gas
    turbine, 50
high-temperature heating pro-
    cesses, 58
hot water space heating, 67
hydro, hydroelectricity, 91, 109
hydro electric power plants (large),
    107
hydrogen fuel cells, 129

I

IC engine power plants, 46
ideal Carnot cycle plant, 52
IEA, 5
India, 13
indicated efficiency, 87

indicated mean effective pressure,
87
industrial heating processses, 57
industrial waste, 10
intake or suction stroke, 81
integrated gasification combined
cycle (IGCC), 44
intercooling, 42
Intergovernmental Panel on Climate Change (IPCC), 95
intermittency, 119
intermittency (of wind power), 114
intermittent operation, 119
internal combustion Diesel engine,
31
internal combustion engines (IC),
28
internal heat demand (domestic),
130
International Energy Agency, (IEA)
5
irreversibilities, 36
irreversible change, 38

J
joule, 1
Joule-Brayton constant pressure
cycle, 40

K
Kelvin-Planck, 21
kilowatt hour, 2
Kyoto protocol, 96

L
La Rance, 118
landfill gas, 10, 113
Laughton, 120
laws of thermodynamics, 19
lignite, 6

losses (heat and work), 131
low temperature heating processes,
59
low utilisation (windmills), 114
low-carbon path, 139

M
major tidal generation scheme, 135
markets for low-carbon technologies, 139
Mauna Los, 94
maximum heat, 29
maximum turbine inlet temperature, 36
maximum work, 41
mean temperature of heat rejection,
35
mean temperature of heat supply,
35
mechanical efficiency, 86
mechanical work, 41
methane, 14
Middle East, 12
mismatch between renewable
generator and grid, 120
mix of fuels, 126
modification of basic IGCC Plant,
45
modifications of basic Rankine
cycle, 35
Mtoe, 2
municipal waste, 10

N
natural gas, 11
new renewables, 18
newton, 1
non-fossil fuel obligation (NFFO),
99
non-flow process, 24

Norway, 108
nuclear fission, 47
nuclear power, 47
nuclear power plant, 46

O

off-shore, 108
off-shore windmills, 108
oil palms, 113
oil shale, 8
on-shore, 108
open circuit gas turbine plant, 37
open cycle gas turbine, 38
open system, 30
Open University (OU), 1, 92
operational and maintenance costs,
    50
Otto constant volume (air standard)
    cycle, 82
overall efficiency, 82
overall energy efficiency, 131
overall flight efficiency, 88
overall thermal efficiency, 86

P

papermaking, 68
pass- out turbine, 68
passive solar, 10
passive solar heating, 107
perfect heat engine, 21
Performance and Innovation Unit
    (PIU), 133
performance of IC engines, 85
perpetual motion machine of the
    second kind (PMMSK), 21
phosphoric acid fuel cell, 49
photosynthesis, 93
photovoltaics, 10
plant utilisation, 59, 81

plant utilisation (hours per annum),
    50, 141
pollution, 91
PMMFK perpetual motion ma-
    chine (first kind), 21
PMMSK perpetual motion ma-
    chine (seond kind), 21
population, 124
power, 2, 19
power for aircraft, 79
power for transport, 79
power plants, 33
ppmv, parts per million by volume,
    94
practical open gas turbine power
    plant, 42
pre-combustion separation, 104
preheating, 56
pressure level at which the steam is
    raised in the boiler, 36
pressure-specific volume diagram,
    40
pressurised water reactors, 47
pressurised fluidised beds (PFBC),
    57
pricing of electricity from CHP
    plants, 75
primary energy, 3, 54
primary energy (contirbution by
    renewables), 111
primary energy consumption mix,
    128
primary energy for transport, 80
primary energy per capita, 124
primary energy supplied, 130
primary energy use (breakdown),
    54
Princeton "wedge" concepts, 136
Princeton University environmental
    research group, 136

Princeton wedge table, 137
processes with chemical change, 24
producing power for transport, 79
propulsive efficiency, 88
propulsive work, 88
proven reserves, 5
proven resources, 6
pulverised coal (PC) boilers, 57
pumping power, 88
PV photovoltaics, 9

R

Rankine cycle, 26, 27
Rankine heat engine, 33
rape, 113
rate of economic growth (high),
    127
rate of supply of energy in fuel,
    142
rating of plant (kW), 141
rational efficiency, 28
RCEP Royal Commission on
    Environmental Pollution, 105,
    125
RCEP scenario, 128
reciprocating internal combustion
    (IC) engine, 80
reduction in carbon emissions
    (60%), 128
reduction in primary energy, 131
reference case, 125
reforestation, 14
refrigeration and air conditioning,
    62
regenerative feed heating, 36
regional and national scenarios,
    127
reheating, 41
renewable biomass sources, 9

renewable electricity generation, 9,
    109, 110
renewable energy, 9, 107
renewable generation expansion, 11
renewable heating systems, 108
renewable power plants, 49
renewable resources, 9
renewables contribution to primary
    energy, 111
required heat, 130
reserves production ratio (R/P), 7
resources, 11
reversibility, 21
reversible heat engine, 23
reversible process, 23
Royal Commission on Environ-
    mental Pollution (RCEP), 135

S

scavenge process, 81
scenario studies, 123
scenarios, 11
Scottish hydro electricity, 108
Severn tidal barrage, 118, 140
Severn Tidal Power group, 118
shaft work, 19
simple open gas turbine plant, 37
Sizewell B power station output,
    128
solar heating, 10, 130
solar photovoltaics (PV), 119
soya beans, 113
spark ignition (SI) engine, 80
specific fuel consumption, 88
stabilisation of carbon emissions,
    136
stationary power plants, 33
steady flow, 25
steam power plant, 33
steam turbine, 33

Stern report, 138
storage schemes (carbon dioxide),
    104
substantial savings in energy costs
    (solar heating), 109
sugar cane, 113
sulphur dioxide, 91
super-critical level, 36
supply modification, 126
syngas, 45
system, 20

T

Tasmania, 108
taxation, 100
technology policy, 138
temperatures on the planet, 14
test discount rate, 143
TFC (total energy for consump-
    tion), 3
thermal efficiecny, 37, 42, 70
thermal efficiency of practical gas
    turbine plants, 42
thermal or thermodynamic effi-
    ciency, 30
thermal radiation, 92
thermal reactors, 47
thermodynamics, 19,
    second law, 20
thrust, 88
tidal, 118
tidal barrages, 118, 135
tidal stream turbines, 118
TPES, (total primary energy sup-
    plied), 3
traditional fuels, 54
traditional renewable biomass, 10
traditional renewables, 108
transport energy demand, 80
transportability of liquid fuels, 79

transportation, 79
turbine cooling, 42
turbojet engine, 88
two-stroke Diesel power plant, 83
two-stroke engine, 81

U

UK actions, 133
ultimately recoverable reserves, 7
UK Royal Commission on Envi-
    ronmental Pollution (RCEP,
    UK), 105, 128
unconventional oil, 8
unfired HRSG, 72
unit cost of fuel ($/kWh), 142
unit price of electricity, 142
United States, 99
unitised production cost, 50, 142
units, 2
uranium, 8
useful heat, 17
useful work, 17
utilisation, 15
utilisation factor, 131

V

van Ohain, 79
vapour compression cycle, 64
variability of loads (diurnal and
    seasonal), 67
variations on the simple open gas
    turbine plant, 41
visual impact of windmills, 114

W

waste, 113
waste (municipal and industrial),
    113
waste heat boiler (WHB), 72

waste products of nuclear fission,
    47
water vapour, 92
water wheels, 9
water-wall riser tubes, 56
watt, 2
wave, 9, 119
wave power, 119
weather (effect on wind power),
    116
Whittle, 79
wind, 114
wind energy distribution, 117
wind power, 114
wind speed, 116

wind turbines, 115
windmills, 114
windpower, 116, 117
windpower (advantages), 114
windpower (disadvantages), 114
wood, 18
work, 1, 14
working or power stroke, 81
world energy consumption, 4, 6, 7,
    11, 13, 14, 128
World Energy Council (WEC) ,
    125
world energy scenarios, 4
world population, 130
world's primary energy, 28